HOUSE
PLANTS

HOUSE
PLANTS

PAUL WILLIAMS

LONDON, NEW YORK, MUNICH,
MELBOURNE, DELHI

SENIOR EDITOR Helen Fewster
PROJECT ART EDITOR Rachael Smith
MANAGING EDITOR Anna Kruger
MANAGING ART EDITOR Alison Donovan
DTP DESIGNER Louise Waller
PICTURE RESEARCH Lucy Claxton, Richard Dabb,
Myriam Megharbi
EDITORIAL ASSISTANT Katie Dock
PRODUCTION CONTROLLER Sarah Sherlock
NORTH AMERICAN EDITOR Christine Heilman

Photography by
SIAN IRVINE

First American Edition, 2006
Text copyright © 2006 Paul Williams

DK Publishing, Inc.
375 Hudson Street
New York, New York 10014

06 07 08 09 10   10 9 8 7 6 5 4 3 2 1

A Cataloging-in-Publication record for this book
is available from the Library of Congress.

ISBN 0-7566-1342-6

SD182
Color reproduction by RGB, Italy
Printed and bound in China by Hung Hing

Discover more at
www.dk.com

Contents

Plant chooser   *6–13*

Introduction   *14-16*

A–Z of plants   *17-172*

Design features
  Statements with shape   *32-33*
  Tricks with texture   *46-47*
  Effects with repetition   *60-61*
  Group impact   *74-75*
  Climbers and trailers   *88-89*
  Natural air fresheners   *102-103*
  Plants for bathrooms   *116-117*
  Low light conditions   *130-131*
  Conservatory plants   *144-145*
  Chill-proof plants   *158-159*

Plant care   *173-174*

Index   *189-191*

Acknowledgments   *192*

Plant chooser | Flowers and berries

Flowering plants

Impatiens p.104

Exacum p.83

Hibiscus p.97

Streptocarpus p.162

Justicia p.107

Saintpaulia p.146

Mandevilla p.113

Campanula p.44

Anthurium p.28

Pericallis p.132

Punica p.141

Pelargonium p.127

Abutilon p.18

Clivia p.56

Brugmansia p.38

Lantana p.110

THERE'S A HOUSEPLANT for almost every situation; this visual guide is designed to help you find one that fits your requirements quickly and easily. Whether you're looking for colorful foliage, scented flowers, something for your bathroom or conservatory, a little winter cheer, or a near-indestructible cactus, the Plant Chooser will point you in the right direction.

Winter features

Solanum p.153

Capsicum p.45

Cyclamen p.66

Rhododendron p.143

Hippeastrum p.98

Schlumbergera p.149

Euphorbia pulcherrima p.81

Camellia p.43

Scented flowers

Lavandula p.111

Gardenia p.91

Stephanotis p.161

Jasminum p.106

Orchids

Phalaenopsis p.133

Paphiopedilum p.125

Dendrobium p.71

Cymbidium p.67

Plant chooser | Interesting foliage

Patterned foliage

Pilea p.137

Solenostemon p.155

Ctenanthe p.62

Begonia pp.34–35

Calathea pp.40–41

Caladium p.39

Stromanthe p.163

Maranta p.114

Texture

Nertera p.121

Gynura p.94

Davallia p.70

Selaginella p.151

Colored leaves

Hypoestes p.101

Hemigraphis p.96

Tradescantia spathacea p.167

Fittonia p.90

Dramatic shape

Codiaeum p.57

Cycas p.65

Nolina p.122

Platycerium p.138

Aechmea p.21

Euphorbia trigona p.82

Air fresheners

Ficus sagittata pp.86–87

Spathiphyllum p.160

Hedera p.95

Chlorophytum p.52

Aglaonema p.24

Dieffenbachia p.72

Syngonium p.164

Dracaena pp.76–77

Plant chooser | Plant specialties

Climbers and trailers

Epipremnum p.80

Senecio rowleyanus p.152

Hedera p.95

Cissus p.54

Hoya p.100

Passiflora p.126

Senecio macroglossus p.152

Cacti and succulents

Ferocactus p.85

Sedum p.150

Agave p.23

Echeveria p.79

Euphorbia tirucalli p.82

Aeonium p.22

Zamioculcas p.171

Aloe p.26

3 1833 04637 528 0

Large plants

Yucca p.170

Curcuma p.64

Ficus binnendijkii 'Alii' pp.86–87

Philodendron pp.134–135

Monstera p.115

Palms

Phoenix p.136

Howea p.99

Rhapis p.142

Dypsis p.78

Plant chooser | Places to go

Conservatory plants

Ananas p.27

Bougainvillea p.37

Kalanchoe pp.108–109

Musa p.118

Citrus p.55

Olea p.123

Plumbago p.139

Plants for bathrooms

Tillandsia p.165

Asplenium p.31

Pteris p.140

Alocasia p.25

Plants for low light

Cyrtomium p.69

Sansevieria p.147

Aspidistra p.30

Adiantum p.20

Cold-tolerant plants

Graptopetalum p.92

Soleirolia p.154

Tolmiea p.166

Isolepsis p.105

Ceropegia p.49

Cordyline p.58

Fatsia p.84

Crassula p.59

Zantedeschia p.172

Schefflera p.148

Grevillea p.93

Sparrmannia p.157

Pachira p.124

Sollya p.156

Introduction

Most of us get satisfaction from being involved with nature in some way. Houseplants bring nature indoors, and at the same time you can take things one step farther by making them important design elements in the home. There's a plant to satisfy everyone's style and taste, and the benefits are well documented: not only do houseplants brighten up your interior, but they can help reduce stress, and also remove volatile chemicals from the air.

This book is a personal selection of reliable, effective plants, but it represents only a fraction of those available from florists, garden centers, and home improvement stores. Once bitten by the houseplant bug, you'll find plenty of others to try. Golden rules? Take time to consider what conditions you have to offer and which plants will grow under those conditions, and you are well on your way to having healthy, good-looking plants that take up a minimum of your time but provide maximum pleasure.

Floral displays immediately brighten up your living room, adding instant color and sometimes scent.

Group arrangements bring extra benefits to your indoor plants. When you position plants with similar needs in close proximity, they work together to create the right level of moisture in the air.

Even simple plants can become stunning and stylish design features—be inventive with your displays.

Just by being there, a plant can improve air quality and make your indoor environment a healthier place. The common spider plant is easy to grow, and research has shown that it is particularly useful at purifying the atmosphere by filtering out common household pollutants.

It's best to choose your plants to suit your site if you want them to thrive.

The range of plants available changes constantly, giving you endless scope to transform your interior.

Using this book

If you're looking for a plant with a particular feature, or for specific conditions, turn to the Plant Chooser for inspiration. There you'll find a pictorial selection, and the page reference will take you straight to the main entry. At the back, there is an expanded, unillustrated version of this list.

In the A–Z section you'll find brief descriptions of around 150 plants, listed in alphabetical order by their botanical names. I have broken down the information into categories to help you make sure the plant suits your conditions. Watering and Survival Strategy are fairly self-explanatory, but some of the others contain generalizations that demand a little explanation.

Light is tricky to define without getting into the technicalities of lux ratings and light meters. There are many variables: the level is dictated by how far north or south you are, and there is a significant difference in the quality of winter and summer light. North-, south-, east- and west-facing windows all receive varying amounts of light at different strengths. Here, "good light" is taken to mean bright light, but not direct sun. Many plants tolerate a weaker direct morning or afternoon sun but not midday heat.

Temperature Normal room temperature is defined as 64–75°F (18–24°C). This is a general definition, and many plants tolerate a few degrees either side of that range.

Size You can often buy plants in a range of sizes; some bigger than shown here, and others smaller. The measurement given on the page is the overall height of the plant and pot illustrated. Large plants are listed in the category index on pp.188–190.

Site Throughout the book I have suggested ways or places to display each plant. These examples are entirely subjective and by no means exhaustive, but are offered as pointers to a suitable site, assuming the light and temperature conditions are met.

At the end of the book I have provided a short practical section offering general advice on plant care. Most plants are prone to at least one or two common pests and diseases, and these, as well as routine problems, are fully covered to help you find out what may have gone wrong, and how to put it right.

A–Z of plants

Abutilon × hybridum
Flowering maple

Abutilons are easy plants for cool, light conditions. Substantial bell-shaped flowers in a range of colors, from deep red to orange, yellow, and pink, are produced during summer and into fall, and the maple-leaf foliage has its own appeal. *A. pictum* 'Thompsonii' has netted variegated leaves; the patterning is caused by a virus, but it is not readily spread to other plants and does little to slow their vigor. Given enough warmth, the evergreens keep growing all year— make sure you provide plenty of light to satisfy any growth stimulated by high temperatures, or your plants will become weak, pale, and drawn.

A. pictum 'Thompsonii'

HOW MUCH LIGHT
Abutilons enjoy full sun, but make sure you keep them moist at the roots to avoid scorching.

ROOM TEMPERATURE
Winter lows of a few degrees above freezing will be tolerated, but cool rooms, 61–68°F (16–20°C), are ideal.

WHEN TO WATER
In warm environments, keep the soil moist year-round. If winters are cooler, reduce the amount of water and allow soil to dry slightly between waterings. Provide balanced liquid fertilizer every two weeks when the plant is in active growth, but stop feeding in winter.

SURVIVAL STRATEGY
Keep plants within bounds by cutting back hard in spring; if you pinch out the growing tips at the same time, you'll get a bushier plant, but it may delay flowering slightly. Growth can be vigorous in summer, so you may need to prune again in early fall. Look out for whitefly (see p.187).

SIZE
22 in/55 cm

SITE
Conservatory; south-facing window

Acalypha hispida

Chenille plant

Acalyphas are bushy plants grown for their foliage and fluffy catkins. *A. hispida* has toothed leaves and red catkins that extend up to 16 in (40 cm) and appear on and off all summer. The plant may grow to 5 ft (1.5 m), but you can keep it small by cutting it back in spring or fall. Speckled varieties of *A. wilkesiana*, with red, green, purple, and copper coloring, may be an acquired taste, but those with single-colored leaves and contrasting margins are indeed handsome.

HOW MUCH LIGHT
For good flowers and foliage color, provide bright, filtered light, such as you might get through a net curtain.

ROOM TEMPERATURE
Acalyphas need a winter minimum of 55–59°F (13–15°C). Lower night temperatures cause leaves to drop.

WHEN TO WATER
During the period of maximum growth, keep the potting mix moist. In the cooler winter months, keep plants on the drier side, but do not allow the soil to dry out completely.

SURVIVAL STRATEGY
Acalyphas enjoy humid conditions: grow two or three together, or with other plants, to help maintain high levels of local humidity. When the weather is particularly warm, your plants will benefit from a regular spray of water on their foliage.

SIZE
14 in/35 cm

SITE
Conservatory

Adiantum capillus-veneris

Maidenhair fern

There are several species of adiantum, all coming under the general name of maidenhair ferns, and *A. capillus-veneris* is one of the prettiest—few plants match its delicacy and grace. The arching fronds are divided into fan-shaped, pale green "pinnae" that contrast beautifully with the fine black stems that carry them. It's a useful little plant for many difficult-to-fill spaces around the home, taking low light levels and cooler positions in stride.

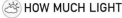
Fronds are made up of fan-shaped "pinnae" (leaflets).

HOW MUCH LIGHT
Keep out of direct sunlight but provide good filtered light.

ROOM TEMPERATURE
Normal room temperature (64–75°F/ 18–24°C) is sufficient, but it will tolerate lows of 50°F (10°C).

WHEN TO WATER
Keep the potting mix just moist throughout the year. The leaves will soon crisp if the roots become dry. The higher the temperature, the greater the need for humidity.

SURVIVAL STRATEGY
Provided you keep it moist, this is an easy plant to grow. If it becomes untidy, you can give your plant a manicure—and a new lease on life— by cutting off all the fronds at the base; it will soon produce a new set. Spring is the best time to do this.

SIZE
16 in/40 cm

SITE
Bathroom

Aechmea fasciata

Vase plant

A striking South American plant from the forest floor, whose dramatic foliage forms a natural "urn," designed to catch rain dripping from above. Its small blue flowers (which turn red) are short-lived, but the bracts last a lot longer. Each rosette has just one flower head, but it dies back slowly: plants look good for months after flowering while new rosettes develop to replace old.

Showy bracts are visible for up to two months

☁ HOW MUCH LIGHT
Good light is essential for flowering: it will tolerate a few hours of direct sunlight, but not scorching, hot sun.

🌡 ROOM TEMPERATURE
Needs winter minimum of 59°F (15°C) and summer maximum—provided humidity is high—of 81°F (27°C).

✋ WHEN TO WATER
Keep the center of the plant filled with soft water. Empty this out occasionally and refill it with fresh water. Keep the potting mix just moist during summer; in winter, allow it to partially dry out before watering sparingly.

✋ SURVIVAL STRATEGY
Despite its humid, tropical origins, it tolerates a wide range of conditions, but if it's too hot and dry, the leaf tips turn brown. Apply half-strength balanced liquid fertilizer semiweekly in summer. A small pot satisfies a large plant; for stability, choose a clay one, or use a weighty cachepot.

📏 SIZE
24 in/ 60 cm

🏠 SITE
Brightly lit room

Aeonium 'Zwartkop'

Aeonium

This is as close to black as you can get in a houseplant. The dramatic foliage forms fleshy rosettes at the end of bare, snake-like stems—combine it with hard steel or glass surfaces for a sharp minimalist look. Large heads of small bright yellow flowers may be produced in early summer. It is easy to grow, with no particular temperature requirements, but good light is essential. Light deficiency causes leaves to elongate and become greener, leading to open, straggly rosettes. It can take full sun, or live outside in summer. Use a heavy pot to give tall plants stability.

HOW MUCH LIGHT
Requires maximum light all year, even in winter when growth stops and plants are virtually dormant.

ROOM TEMPERATURE
Prefers cool winters, around 46–52°F (8–11°C); in summer, temperatures of 64–77°F (18–25°C) suffice.

WHEN TO WATER
Keep soil moist in summer, to keep foliage from flagging. In winter, reduce watering but water if leaves drop or lose their shine. Give a half-strength balanced liquid fertilizer every month in summer and nothing in winter. Keep water off the foliage: it leaves an unsightly white deposit.

SURVIVAL STRATEGY
Old leaves shrivel and fall: this is normal. Tall, bare-stemmed plants can be cut back hard. It takes nerve to cut most of your plant off, but you will end up with a nicer shape, and you can root the rosettes you remove in moist gritty potting mix. Vine weevil can be a nuisance (see p.187).

SIZE
20 in/50 cm

SITE
Minimalist interior

Agave attenuata

Agave

Agaves are tough, strongly-shaped plants, ideal for the bright sunshine and heat of a conservatory. They make good, architectural specimen plants. *A. attenuata* develops a sturdy trunk. The more common *A. americana* forms a rosette with broad, spiny-edged leaves that can eventually grow very large. There are also smaller, slower-growing species: *A. filifera* has wispy white threads edging its leaves, and stocky *A. victoriae-reginae*, which is no higher than 10 in (25 cm) and makes a compact rosette of leaves with bright white marks.

HOW MUCH LIGHT
Provide as much light as possible throughout the year.

ROOM TEMPERATURE
Agaves are tolerant of low winter temperatures of around 41–43°F (5–6°C) if they are kept dry.

WHEN TO WATER
During active growth, water regularly, getting the potting mix moist but letting it partly dry out between waterings. In winter, keep just enough moisture in the soil to stop it from drying completely.

SURVIVAL STRATEGY
Undemanding plants with no special needs. Some have very sharp, spiny tips that can be dangerous to children's eyes—trim them off with nail clippers, or skewer wine corks on the tips. New plants are often bundled up for transport; the leaves will spread and flatten out with time.

SIZE
22 in/ (56 cm)

SITE
Contemporary interior

Aglaonema commutatum

Aglaonema

Large leaves splashed and marked in greens, grays, and cream and a fairly tough constitution make aglaonemas easy and attractive houseplants. Hybrids and selections of several species have given rise to a large number of varieties with leaf size varying from 6–16 in (15–40 cm) long, and innumerable leaf patterns. All enjoy similar conditions and treatment. Aglaonemas will grow in shade, but provide them with plenty of light to encourage good leaf markings.

A. crispum 'Marie'

☼ HOW MUCH LIGHT
Keep out of direct light to avoid scorching the leaves.

🌡 ROOM TEMPERATURE
Normal room temperature, 64–75°F (18–24°C).

💧 WHEN TO WATER
Water regularly, allowing the potting mix to dry slightly between waterings. When growth slows during winter, reduce watering accordingly, but do not allow it to dry out completely.

✋ SURVIVAL STRATEGY
Plants benefit from a semiweekly balanced liquid fertilizer when they are in active growth. A dry atmosphere causes browning of the leaf edges and tips, so stand the plant on a tray of moist pebbles to raise humidity if your air is dry.

📏 SIZE
20 in/ 48 cm

🏠 SITE
Airy kitchen

Alocasia x *amazonica*

Elephant ear

Alocasias are not the easiest plants to grow because of their need for humidity and constantly warm conditions, but if you succeed, you will have a spectacular plant with large leaves ribbed and marked in a most dramatic fashion. On a well grown plant, leaves reach 20 in (50 cm) long—or more. Cool conditions cause the leaves to drop, but if the temperature is restored within a day or two, new foliage will be produced from the underground rhizome.

HOW MUCH LIGHT
Keep out of direct sunlight but provide bright filtered light.

ROOM TEMPERATURE
Maintain winter minimum of 59–64°F (15–18°C); in summer, temperatures of 68–77°F (20–25°C) are ideal.

WHEN TO WATER
Water regularly during the summer months, keeping the potting mix moist. During winter, reduce watering.

SURVIVAL STRATEGY
Feed weekly when actively growing; stop feeding during winter. Reasonably high humidity is important. Regular spraying and standing plants on a tray of damp pebbles will help. Use soft water when spraying to avoid leaving unsightly deposits on leaves.

SIZE
24 in/60 cm

SITE
Bright bathroom

Aloe variegata

Partridge-breast aloe

There are many kinds of aloe, and all are easy to grow. *A. variegata* is tough and smaller than most, making it an ideal houseguest. Spikes of tubular red flowers emerge in spring and early summer, but its robust foliage looks good all year. *A. vera*'s reputation as a healer ensures a welcome on windowsills around the world. It forms a rosette of upright, succulent leaves, spotted pale white with toothed edges, and produces tall spikes of yellow flowers. For even more tactile effects, try *A. aristata*, whose compact rosette is comprised of fleshy leaves dashed with knobby tubercules, and sends up typical orange aloe flowers on 12-in (30-cm) stalks in summer.

A. aristata (Lace aloe)

HOW MUCH LIGHT
Aloes need good light year-round. They tolerate full sun, but keep them out of very hot midday summer sun.

ROOM TEMPERATURE
Ideal range is 64–75°F (18–24°C). For flowers, provide a 4–5-week chilling (as low as 50°F/10°C) in winter.

WHEN TO WATER
Take care to keep water out of the tightly packed foliage. In summer, keep the soil just moist; in winter, keep it on the dry side, but do not allow it to dry out completely. Apply a half-strength balanced liquid fertilizer every 2 weeks during summer. Stop feeding in winter.

SURVIVAL STRATEGY
Aloes are easily cared for: simply provide plenty of light and ensure they are not overwatered. They often produce offsets, which you can cut off and pot in a free-draining, loam-based potting mix.

SIZE
27 in/
67 cm

SITE
Sunny windowsill

Ananas comosus var. *variegatus*

Pineapple

A striking plant that may, unfortunately, become too big for most homes, but it is spectacularly showy if you have the space. It's a variegated form of the edible pineapple, with bold narrow leaves up to 36 in (90 cm) long, toothed and edged with a broad creamy-white stripe. If you have room, try combining it with other bromeliads, such as bilbergias and aechmeas, to create a themed display of rich textures and dramatic shapes.

In direct sunlight, leaf margins acquire a pink tinge.

☼ HOW MUCH LIGHT
Ananas does not have a resting period, so it needs as much direct sunlight as possible all year.

🌡 ROOM TEMPERATURE
Keep warm year-round, with a winter minimum of 61°F (16°C).

☂ WHEN TO WATER
A. comosus grows year-round, so water frequently in summer and keep the potting mix just moist during winter. The cooler the winter temperature, the drier the plant should be kept.

✋ SURVIVAL STRATEGY
Given a warm temperature, good light, moderate humidity, and a free-draining bromeliad mix, this is a straightforward plant to care for. Unfortunately, the fruit takes several months to mature and is unlikely to reach any great size or even be edible when grown indoors.

▯ SIZE
14 in/
36 cm

⌂ SITE
Conservatory

Anthurium hybrids
Flamingo flower

There are a number of species of anthurium; many are very large and usually grown as cut flowers for florists. But for the home, breeders have produced compact plants that are more tolerant of household conditions. Their shiny white, pink, or red flowers appear intermittently throughout the year, but even when out of flower, it makes an attractive foliage plant. The flowers have a presence all of their own, so give your plant a prominent position. Anthuriums are best displayed individually in a simple but stylish pot that does not attempt to compete with the flowers.

A. 'Champion'

HOW MUCH LIGHT
Provide strong but indirect light in summer; during winter, when the sun is weaker, it will enjoy full light.

ROOM TEMPERATURE
The winter minimum is 61°F (16°C), but a year-round constant of around 68°F (20°C) is preferable.

WHEN TO WATER
A tricky customer. Never allow the potting mix to dry out, but also avoid continually soggy soil, since this will damage the roots.

SURVIVAL STRATEGY
This is not the easiest plant to grow because it needs constant conditions of temperature and humidity. It will not tolerate drafts, so position it away from doors or open windows. Raise humidity by spraying regularly.

SIZE
22 in/
56 cm

SITE
Bathroom

Asparagus densiflorus 'Myersii'

Foxtail fern

Despite its common name, this is not a fern—although with its soft and fluffy foliage, it could understandably be taken for one at first glance. It is a tough plant with large tuberous water-storing roots that give it a degree of resilience to drying out and make it much more tolerant of heat and drought than many true ferns. A well grown plant makes a good bushy mound of light green foliage on upright stems 16 in (40 cm) long. It is ideal as a foil for larger leaves or as soft background for brightly flowered plants. For an elegant and slightly Asian look, consider the fine, wispy leaves and tiered stems of *A. setaceus*. Young plants are small and bushy, but as they mature, they reveal that their real inclination is to climb—by sending out long shoots and scrambling up to 10 ft (3 m) in height. If space is an issue, *A. setaceus* 'Nanus' stays small and compact.

A. setaceus

HOW MUCH LIGHT
Provide plenty of bright light but avoid direct sunlight.

ROOM TEMPERATURE
Tolerates lows of 45°F (7°C), happier at 61–70°F (16–21°C). *A. setaceus* needs warmer winters (55°F/13°C).

WHEN TO WATER
Water both *A. densiflorus* and *A. setaceus* regularly during summer, keeping the potting mix continually moist but not wet. Reduce watering during winter, so soil is only just moist. If *A. setaceus* becomes dry, its fine leaves will quickly turn brown.

SURVIVAL STRATEGY
Undernourished plants become a pale and sickly-looking green, so apply a balanced liquid fertilizer regularly during summer. If plants become congested (or if you just want more), divide in spring by splitting apart the dense mass of tubers and potting the divisions.

SIZE
20 in/ 49 cm

SITE
Bathroom; hanging basket

Aspidistra elatior

Cast-iron plant

The aspidistra has almost become a victim of its own success: because it can withstand considerable neglect, it gets considerably neglected, and many specimens are seen stuck in a dark corner, covered in dust and bone dry, but still alive—a cast-iron constitution indeed. But give it good potting mix and regular fertilizing and you will be rewarded with an impressive show of broad, dark green, healthy foliage. There is a variegated form, too: make sure you provide it with good light to make the most of the special effects.

A. elatior 'Variegata'

HOW MUCH LIGHT
Although they cope with shade, aspidistras grow better in good light—but keep out of direct sunlight.

ROOM TEMPERATURE
Tolerates temperatures just above freezing, but happiest at room temperature, 64–75°F (18–24°C).

WHEN TO WATER
Keep the pottiing mix just moist and water regularly during the warm summer growing season. Brown spots on leaves are usually a sign of overwatering.

SURVIVAL STRATEGY
Not a fussy plant and easily grown with minimum attention. Keep the leaves clean by wiping them with a damp cloth. Throughout summer, provide a balanced liquid fertilizer every 3 weeks.

SIZE
33 in/82 cm

SITE
Minimalist interior; shady hallway

Asplenium nidus
Bird's-nest fern

Here is a fern that's traveling incognito: it is not immediately recognizable because unlike most ferns, the fronds are not divided. Entire, shiny pale green fronds unroll from the center of the rosette and expand, often with wavy edges, to form a "bowl" or "nest" that can be as much as 3 ft (1 m) across, though it's often much less. Because of its architectural shape and light green coloring, it is a good plant for creating a bold, leafy jungle effect. Try it alongside calatheas or aspidistras.

Young fronds unfurl from the center of the plant.

HOW MUCH LIGHT
Direct sun is likely to cause leaves to scorch, so provide dappled shade.

ROOM TEMPERATURE
The winter minimum is 55°F (13°C), but year-round temperatures of 64–75°F (18–24°C) are better.

WHEN TO WATER
Keep the potting mix well watered through the growing season. During winter periods of no growth, keep the soil just moist.

SURVIVAL STRATEGY
Young fronds are quite tender and scorch easily in hot sun. Provide a balanced liquid fertilizer every 3 weeks through the growing period, but stop during the winter months when no growth occurs. Clean leaves with a damp cloth, but take care: fronds are easily damaged.

SIZE
15 in/38 cm

SITE
Brightly lit kitchen

YOU DON'T NEED FLOWERS TO SAY IT WITH PLANTS: many will never flower indoors, but more than compensate with the bold shapes created by their leaves and stems. Choose a plant with a strong architectural shape or a distinctive form and you can give a room a new focal point, or make a dramatic statement with astonishing ease.

Isolepsis cernua **p.105**

Euphorbia trigona **p.82**

Agave attenuata **p.23**

Begonia Rex-cultorum 'Fireworks'

Begonia

There is a begonia to suit almost any situation and taste, from bright and colorful flowery hybrids to sophisticated plants with striking foliage; from small plants 1 in (2–3 cm) high to those well over 3 ft (1 m). Those known as Rex-cultorum hybrids have some of the most dramatic foliage. Many have large leaves veined or marked with bold patterns of silver, purple, green, or red—and often accessorized with colorful hairy stems. Whether you see them more as flowers or foliage plants, this is a great plant group to explore.

LEAF CUTTINGS Plant a leaf with a 1 in (2.5 cm) stalk so it rests on the soil surface. A plastic bag helps raise humidity. New plants form in about 2 months.

HOW MUCH LIGHT
Most begonias enjoy bright light away from scorching sunshine.

ROOM TEMPERATURE
Despite their wide variety, begonias all require temperatures around 64–70°F (18–21°C).

WHEN TO WATER
Plants with congested or hairy stems are best watered from below to prevent rotting in their crown.

SURVIVAL STRATEGY
Remove fallen flowers, especially on winter-flowering plants: if left lying on the foliage, they will cause rotting. Begonia mildew can be a problem on the leaves of some varieties if the plants are under stress from drought or heat. Remove affected leaves and use a suitable fungicide.

SIZE
13 in/33 cm

SITE
Living room

Other varieties

B. hatacoa 'Silver' Compact and cool with white flowers adding to the effect. Mildew may be hard to spot. To 12 in (30 cm) tall.

B. 'Rieger Hybrid' Winter bloomers provide cheerful color from fall to spring but are susceptible to mildew. To 16 in (40 cm).

B. benichoma Striking, mildew-resistant plant with leaves divided into several leaflets atop long upright stems 16–20 in (40–50 cm) tall.

◁ *B.* 'Red Robin' has ribbed, crinkled, and hairy leaves whose deep red coloring is encouraged by good light. To 10 in (25 cm).

Calathea makoyana
Peacock plant

Although calatheas are not the easiest plants to grow, they're certainly not beyond the skills of an enthusiast. Their appeal rests with the astonishing patterns and veining that many display, and the dark colors of the foliage undersides. Some have lacy, see-through leaves; others are robust and boldly decorated. They associate well with one another, but are equally at home mixing with ferns and other plants that enjoy lightly shaded conditions, and as foils for more flowery plants. With the exception of *C. crocata*, their own flowers are not showy and unlikely to be produced inside.

Stunning patterns explain common name.

☼ HOW MUCH LIGHT
Keep out of direct sunshine but provide bright filtered light.

🌡 ROOM TEMPERATURE
Ideally, maintain year-round levels of around 68°F (20°C) and do not allow to drop significantly in winter.

☝ WHEN TO WATER
Water regularly with soft water, keeping the potting mix moist but not wet in summer. Reduce watering in winter when growth is slower. Keep humidity as high as you can: the warmer the temperature, the higher it should be.

🖐 SURVIVAL STRATEGY
Protect plants from drafts. Dust spoils the appearance: carefully swish the leaves of an upturned plant in a bowl of lukewarm water to clean it. Hot, dry conditions are the enemy, but keep them out of direct sun and moist at the roots and your calatheas will thrive.

🗋 SIZE
23 in/57 cm

🏠 SITE
Bathroom; shady living room

C. 'Blue Grass' provides lush, fresh-green arching foliage, despite its name, for a shady spot in a humid atmosphere.

C. crocata needs warmth and humidity but is doubly ornamental with flamboyant flowers and dark foliage with purple undersides.

C. majestica copes with low light levels—as its dark foliage testifies. The robust near-black leaves are streaked with white or pink lines.

◁ *C. rufibarba* makes hearty, upright clumps of red-and-green wavy-edged foliage. Look out for red spider mite in dry atmospheres.

Callisia repens

Callisia

This is a busy little plant with small leaves reminiscent of its close relative, *Tradescantia*. It is a creeping plant that you can use either on its own as a trailer—its long stems extend to 20 in (50 cm)—or to cover the surface beneath other plants in larger pots. It also provides good groundcover for conservatory beds. Small white flowers are produced, usually in late summer. *Callisia elegans*, the striped inch plant, has larger foliage with white stripes.

HOW MUCH LIGHT
Provide bright light, ideally with a few hours of early morning or late afternoon sunlight.

ROOM TEMPERATURE
Normal room temperatures, 64–75°F (18–24°C), are best, with a winter minimum of 50°F (10°C).

WHEN TO WATER
Keep the potting mix moist when the plant is in active growth. During the winter resting period, allow it to dry out slightly between waterings. Provide a dose of half-strength balanced liquid fertilizer every two weeks.

SURVIVAL STRATEGY
Don't be afraid to trim this plant back if it becomes straggly. Shearing over with scissors stimulates new shoots and freshens up tired-looking plants. Push the pieces you cut off into moist potting mix and put in a shady spot, and they will soon root.

SIZE
10 in/25 cm

SITE
East- or west-facing windowsill

Camellia japonica 'Mary Williams'
Camellia

This handsome evergreen woody shrub has glossy, dark green, leathery leaves that make the perfect foil for its large, showy flowers. Double or single pink, white, or crimson flowers are produced in late winter and spring. It eventually makes a shrub too large for most homes; in mild areas, plant it in the garden in neutral or acidic soil when it reaches this stage. The flower buds are initiated and start to develop between midsummer and early fall; it is important not to let the plant dry out during this period or the buds will fall off before they have fully opened. Camellias enjoy cool conditions. In warm environments, the flowers will be shorter-lived and, in the long term, growth may be straggly.

C. japonica 'Lovelight'

C. japonica 'Jupiter'

☁ HOW MUCH LIGHT
Requires bright light, but keep out of direct sunlight.

🌡 ROOM TEMPERATURE
Withstands 23°F (−5°C), but the ideal range is 61–70°F (16–21°C) in summer and 50–61°F (10–16°C) in winter.

✋ WHEN TO WATER
Use soft water and keep the plant just moist during the winter period. Water well throughout summer. After flowering, provide a balanced liquid fertilizer suitable for acid-loving plants until late summer.

✋ SURVIVAL STRATEGY
Grow camellias in ericaceous (nonalkaline) compost. Keep the plant within bounds by pruning just after flowering. Look out for black sooty mold on the leaves; this indicates the presence of aphids or scale insects (see p.187).

📏 SIZE
36 in/90 cm

🏠 SITE
Cool, well-lit hallway

Campanula isophylla

Star-of-Bethlehem

Few trailing plants can boast as much flower power as these blue- or white-flowered campanulas. In spring and summer, each stem produces great quantities of flower buds which, when fully open, completely hide the foliage. Be warned: high summer temperatures cause flowers to fade and plants to become open and straggly. Once flowering is over, move the plant to cool winter quarters, such as a cold greenhouse or conservatory.

HOW MUCH LIGHT
Keep out of hot, direct sunlight, but provide good light to keep the plant compact.

ROOM TEMPERATURE
Winter lows of 36–50°F (2–10°C) are essential for good flowering. Warm winters will result in fewer flowers.

WHEN TO WATER
Water regularly in summer, keeping soil moist but not wet. Keep just moist in winter, and water from below to prevent stems and leaves from getting wet and rotting. Provide a semiweekly dose of balanced liquid fertilizer while plants are in flower; stop when flowering finishes.

SURVIVAL STRATEGY
Pick spent flowers to stop them from rotting on the plant and encourage more blooms. The congested stems provide ideal conditions for fungal diseases like gray mold if the plant is not kept dry enough, or sufficiently well ventilated in winter. Make sure you clean it up before dormancy.

SIZE
11 in/28 cm

SITE
East-facing windowsill

Capsicum annuum Conioides Group

Chili pepper

Ornamental peppers have enduring, bright, showy, fleshy fruits that are long and thin or rounded, or somewhere in between. Colors range from cream, yellow, orange, and red to purple, and change as they ripen, creating a harlequin effect. The small white flowers are insignificant. They are annuals, so discard when the fruits wither. You can raise plants from seed; give them warmth and plenty of light.

C. annuum Cerasiforme Group (cherry pepper)

HOW MUCH LIGHT
Good light with some direct sun is essential—and tricky in winter. Keep it in the brightest spot in the house.

ROOM TEMPERATURE
Room temperatures of 64–75°F (18–24°C) are sufficient, but fruits last longer in cooler conditions.

WHEN TO WATER
Do not let the plant dry out. Keep the potting mix moist, but do not allow it to stand in water. Apply a balanced liquid fertilizer every two weeks.

SURVIVAL STRATEGY
If the fruits fall off, check that your plant is getting sufficient light; that it has not been allowed to dry out; that it is out of cold drafts; and that it has not been overwatered.

SIZE
11 in/28 cm

SITE
Bright kitchen windowsill

Alocasia x *amazonica*, **p.25**; *Calathea* 'Blue Grass', **pp.40–41**

PLANTS HAVE EVOLVED in response to conditions in the wild: hairy leaves protect against heat, cold, or insect attack; thick, fleshy leaves combat drought. With a spectacular range of textures to choose from, you can use plants as you would fabrics for stunning effects. Soften hard edges with fluffy ferns, cheer stark corners with crinkly leaves, or add shine with glossy green foliage.

Sedum morganianum, **p.150**

Gynura aurantiaca, **p.94**

Selaginella martensii 'Watsoniana', **p.151**

Davillia canariensis, **p.70;** *Asparagus setaceus,* **p.29**

Caryota mitis
Fishtail palm

A strange-looking palm that almost looks as if it was never quite finished, or as though its leaves have been attacked by nibbling insects. Its odd un-palmlike habit makes it a curiosity and a good talking point, even though some may argue that it is not the most beautiful of plants. But for me, a large specimen has an almost sinister presence that I find attractive. It is not fast-growing, so if you want a large one, it's better to buy big than to wait for a small one to grow. Use it to provide shade for smaller, low-growing foliage plants that enjoy filtered light and share a taste for humidity, such as calatheas and marantas, both of which complement the caryota foliage.

 HOW MUCH LIGHT
Provide as much light as possible, but not direct scorching sunlight.

 ROOM TEMPERATURE
Requires a minimum of 59°F (15°C) all year, but in temperate zones you can place it outside during summer.

 **WHEN TO WATER**
Keep well watered during summer when light and temperature are good. When growth slows in winter, reduce the amount of water, and allow the surface of the potting mix to dry out before watering.

 **SURVIVAL STRATEGY**
The fact that it is native to Burma and Malaya gives some indication that it likes a warm and humid environment. You can encourage a humid atmosphere by standing it on a tray of moist pebbles (see p.178).

 SIZE
5½ ft/1.7 m

 SITE
Airy living room

Ceropegia linearis subsp. *woodii*

Hearts on a string

I like this plant. At a distance, all you might notice is the long—up to 6 ft (2 m)—hanging, wiry stems strung with small, silvery-gray hearts, but close up it is a different story. The surface of each succulent, sea-green heart is patterned with gray and purple, and the underside is a smooth soft pink-purple that just folds around the edge of the leaf to give the textured surface a neat rim. The flowers are small but detailed, and develop into two extraordinarily long needlelike seed pods.

Summer flowers are just ½ in (1–2 cm) long.

 HOW MUCH LIGHT
Provide plenty of direct light or it will develop spindly stems with poor coloring and spaced-out leaves.

ROOM TEMPERATURE
Normal room temperature, 64–75°F (18–24°C), is sufficient, with a winter minimum of 46°F (8°C).

WHEN TO WATER
Keep the potting mix moist but not wet when in active growth. In winter, give it just enough water to prevent wilting or shriveling, but beware of overwatering. Give it a half-strength balanced liquid fertilizer every two weeks during the summer months.

SURVIVAL STRATEGY
This is an undemanding plant. It enjoys direct sunlight and, while it is best kept moist during the growing season, it will stand the occasional drying out. You can use the small tubers, which develop at intervals along the stems, for propagation.

SIZE
24 in/60 cm

SITE
Hanging basket; sunny shelf

Chamaedorea elegans

Parlor palm

This is a very common palm, much used in conservatories, office lobbies, and hotel foyers, which reveals at least one thing: it is tough and easy to grow. It is a leafy plant with several upright stems bearing typical palm leaves that arch over as they get bigger, but it rarely gets taller than 5 ft (1.5 m). Small yellow flowers may be produced, but they are of no real significance. This is an easy-going plant if it is kept out of very dry atmospheres and hot, direct sun, both of which will cause browning of the leaf tips. Keep conservatories well ventilated in summer to prevent stifling temperatures.

HOW MUCH LIGHT
Tolerates shade, but bright, filtered light (not direct, scorching sun) gives you healthier, more compact plants.

ROOM TEMPERATURE
Maintain a winter minimum of 61°F (16°C); otherwise, room temperatures of 64–75°F (18–24°C) are sufficient.

WHEN TO WATER
During the summer months, water freely, keeping the potting mix moist at all times. In the cooler winter months, it needs less water; allow the top of the soil to dry out before further watering.

SURVIVAL STRATEGY
When the plant is growing during summer, provide a balanced liquid fertilizer every 2 weeks. Although it tolerates occasional periods of dry air, it prefers a humid atmosphere, which you can encourage by standing the plant on a tray of moist pebbles and misting regularly.

SIZE
26 in/66 cm

SITE
Hallways or stairwells

Chamaerops humilis
Dwarf fan palm

A tough plant in many respects. The stiff and spiny leaves are most attractive as they unfold their compressed pleats, gradually splitting into fanlike fingers. It grows slowly with either a single stem or several short congested stems, all bearing fans that crisscross and overlap. Over time, it can eventually reach 4 ft (1.2 m) and outgrow the average home, but it tolerates several degrees of frost if it's kept dry, and will sit happily outside in full sun during summer.

MANICURING TIPS Unsightly browning leaves may indicate that your plant has been too hot or left too dry. Continually trim off any damaged or brown tips to keep the foliage looking its best.

HOW MUCH LIGHT
Give it as much light as possible at all times.

ROOM TEMPERATURE
Tolerates frost but 46–50°F (8–10°C) is ideal in winter; prefers 59–75°F (15–24°C) in summer.

WHEN TO WATER
During the summer months, water regularly to keep the potting mix moist. In winter, when growth has stopped, allow the soil to dry out before watering sparingly.

SURVIVAL STRATEGY
This is an easy going plant that copes well with indoor life if you respect its need for good drainage and a light, loam-based potting mix, and avoid overwatering it.

SIZE
34 in/85 cm

SITE
Brightly lit hallway; airy conservatory

Chlorophytum comosum 'Vittatum'

Spider plant

Traditionally one of the most ubiquitous, loved, neglected, and generally abused houseplants, but still one of the best for brightening shady rooms and tolerating harsh treatment. Be fair to the plant; give it proper care and conditions and it will look twice as good as the specimens found languishing in dark corners. The arching yellow stems, which produce small white flowers and end in cascades of miniature plants, are an added bonus.

HOW MUCH LIGHT
As much as possible in winter, when light levels are low, to maintain good leaf color. Avoid scorching sun.

ROOM TEMPERATURE
Normal room temperature, 64–75°F (18–24°C), is adequate, with a winter minimum of 46°F (8°C).

WHEN TO WATER
Keep potting mix moist when the plant is active, from spring to fall. During the winter resting period, reduce watering and allow soil to dry out slightly before watering again. Regular semiweekly doses of balanced liquid fertilizer during the growing period help keep it healthy.

SURVIVAL STRATEGY
Try not to bend the arching leaves: once kinked, they never fully recover and are best cut out low down with scissors. Large, fleshy roots pushing up out of the soil indicate it needs repotting. Brown leaf tips are caused by a dry atmosphere or by dryness at the roots; snip them off.

SIZE
20 in/50 cm

SITE
End table; shady living room

Chrysanthemum cultivars
Chrysanthemum

Potted chrysanthemums are ideal for adding short-term cheer and color to the home. There are plenty to choose from, in a wide range of colors to suit any mood or decor, and the plants themselves are undemanding and long-flowering. Discard old plants. Young, newly bought plants will have been pinched out and treated with a dwarfing agent to keep them neat and compact; they become much taller when the effects wear off. If you want to keep old plants, then put them in the garden in mild weather and let them grow tall.

C. 'Zuki'

☀ HOW MUCH LIGHT
Bright light is needed to encourage buds to open and for healthy growth, but keep out of scorching sunlight.

🌡 ROOM TEMPERATURE
A cool 55–57°F (13–14°C) is best. Warm conditions cause the flowers to open and fade much more quickly.

💧 WHEN TO WATER
Pot chrysanthemums are often grown several to a pot so that you get more leaf and flower per pot; this means they are particularly thirsty and need regular watering. Soak them from the bottom to avoid getting the crown wet or encouraging the leaves to rot.

✋ SURVIVAL STRATEGY
These are temporary guests, so there's no need to feed them. Remove spent flowers to prevent disease and to encourage more buds to open.

📏 SIZE
14 in/35 cm

🏠 SITE
Cool, bright rustic interior

Cissus rhombifolia 'Ellen Danica'

Grape ivy

Strictly speaking, this is a climber that uses its tendrils to travel aloft, and it is readily trained up a trellis, where it will reach a height of 6 ft (2 m). However, you can just as easily use it without support, allowing it to spill out of its pot and trail downward. The foliage is softly hairy when young, which gives the new olive-green leaves a silvery gleam; mature foliage turns a glossy dark green. It's an undemanding plant and tolerates a wide range of conditions.

HOW MUCH LIGHT
For sturdy, compact growth, choose a brightly lit site out of direct midday sun, which is likely to scorch foliage.

ROOM TEMPERATURE
Grow at normal room temperature, 64–75°F (18–24°C), with a winter minimum of 54°F (12°C).

WHEN TO WATER
Water regularly during spring and summer when the plant is actively growing; reduce watering in winter when activity is slower and temperatures are lower. Plants wintering in warm rooms will need more regular watering.

SURVIVAL STRATEGY
You can cut out occasional vigorous shoots at any time, but wait until spring to carry out major cutting back. Regularly tie in shoots to help keep the plant neat and tidy. Provide monthly doses of balanced liquid fertilizer during the growing season. Do not fertilize in winter.

SIZE
36 in/90 cm

SITE
Jungle effect in cool conservatory

x *Citrofortunella microcarpa* syn. *Citrus mitis*

Calamondin orange

This is one of the easier citrus plants to grow. It is quite a charmer, almost guaranteed to add some fruity finishing touches to your home. It's always exciting to grow something that not only looks and smells good, but also offers the chance of edible fruits (they may be a little bitter, but try making your own exclusive jar of marmalade; there is satisfaction to be had from producing a good crop). The scented spring flowers are self-fertile, but give them a dab with a small paintbrush if there are no insects around to shake the pollen up. The plant will benefit from the fresher outdoor environment during summer and, provided it is out of the wind, can be placed outside from early to late summer, avoiding the cold nights of spring and early fall.

KEEPING TRIM Cut back sideshoots and growing tips by about one-third to keep the plant compact and bushy. Do this in spring, before flowering, and cut just above a bud.

HOW MUCH LIGHT
Good bright light is vital for good flowering and compact growth.

ROOM TEMPERATURE
Ideal summers of 72–77°F (22–25°C); takes 57°F (14°C) in winter. Provide higher humidity in warm conditions.

WHEN TO WATER
Water regularly during the growing season, but during winter, when temperatures are lower, let potting mix partially dry out before watering. Feed in spring and early summer with a high-nitrogen fertilizer, then continue with a balanced liquid fertilizer until early fall.

SURVIVAL STRATEGY
A good crop relies on a healthy plant, and that depends on rich potting mix, plenty of fertilizer, warm temperatures, high humidity, and good light. All citrus are sensitive to cold drafts and respond by losing their leaves. Too much or too little water can also lead to leaf-drop.

SIZE
24 in/60 cm

SITE
Conservatory

Clivia miniata
Kaffir lily

This is a robust evergreen, with beefy, straplike, glossy leaves. The large flowers open in a dense head at the top of a thick stalk, usually toward the end of winter and early spring; there may be as many as 15 warm orange, yellow, or apricot flowers in a single head. Clivias enjoy cramped conditions; don't worry about roots pushing out of the top of the pot, but wait until the plant is almost being forced out of its container by the overcrowded roots before repotting. It is difficult to water potbound plants from above, so dunk them in a bucket of water, then allow to drain.

Bursting anthers dust the petals with pollen.

HOW MUCH LIGHT
Give clivias a position in bright light at all times of the year, but keep out of midday sun during summer.

ROOM TEMPERATURE
Prefers cool summers, 64°F (18°C), and a winter resting period at 45–46°F (7–8°C).

WHEN TO WATER
During the growing season, water regularly, keeping the potting mix moist but not wet. In winter, keep watering to a minimum. Feed when the plant is actively growing—which will be when the flower is well formed. Stop fertilizing in late summer.

SURVIVAL STRATEGY
An easy plant to care for, flowering regularly as long as it is given a rest in early winter. Two months of cooler temperatures around 45°F (7°C) and reduced watering will emulate its natural life cycle and bring it into flower at the right time. Too much warmth shortens the flowering span.

SIZE
27 in/68 cm

SITE
Bright living room

Codiaeum variegatum var. *pictum*

Croton

You either love this plant or hate it. The exotic colored leaves and stiff habit are not to everyone's taste, but whatever you think about it, it is certainly hard to miss. Apart from their bright red, orange, green, yellow, and occasionally purple colors, the leaves come in a surprising range of shapes, too, from long and narrow to deeply lobed and contorted. If you have the space, grow it large—up to 3 ft (1 m)—so that its bright colors are balanced by its stature.

C. variegatum var. *pictum* 'Gold Star'

C. variegatum var. *pictum* 'Frank Brown'

HOW MUCH LIGHT
Good light is essential for colors to develop. Likes some direct sun; keep soil moist to prevent scorching.

ROOM TEMPERATURE
Normal room temperature, 64–75°F (18–24°C), is sufficient, with a winter minimum of 55–57°F (13–14°C).

WHEN TO WATER
Water frequently when temperatures are high during summer, keeping the potting mix moist but not wet. In winter, keep the soil only just moist.

SURVIVAL STRATEGY
Apply a balanced liquid fertilizer every two weeks throughout summer. Keep plants small by cutting back in spring, but take care to avoid contact with the white sap, which may irritate and inflame eyes and skin. Do not position these plants in drafts or dry atmospheres.

SIZE
26 in/ 67 cm

SITE
Jazz up minimalist interiors

Cordyline australis

Cabbage palm

This is a versatile plant that in temperate climates can be used indoors or out during summer, and brought back inside for winter. It is grown for its fountain of leaves, which may be purple-brown, green, or variegated with white, red, or yellow. Youngsters are ideal as centerpieces in small foliage arrangements. Larger plants will suit a conservatory, where they can withstand high summer temperatures provided you keep them well-watered.

C. fruticosa 'Red Edge' (good luck tree)

HOW MUCH LIGHT
C. australis does not enjoy shade, so provide as much light as possible, including 2–3 hours of direct sun.

ROOM TEMPERATURE
A normal range of 64–75°F (18–24°C) is ideal, but plants can survive near-freezing temperatures unharmed.

WHEN TO WATER
Keep moist in summer. If winter temperatures are low, water sparingly, keeping the potting mix only just moist.

SURVIVAL STRATEGY
This is an easy-going plant that needs minimal attention. Pull off older leaves as they fade and shrivel. Regularly apply a balanced liquid fertilizer during summer to maintain good leaf color.

SIZE
24 in/60 cm

SITE
Conservatory

Crassula ovata syn. *C. argentea*

Jade plant

Judging from the number of these plants you see around and the dire neglect many of them suffer yet still survive, this must be one of the toughest houseplants available. It has succulent leaves, often with a thin red edge, and a thick, fleshy stem that stores the water that keeps the plant alive when you forget to provide it. Occasionally it produces small white fall flowers. Fans of feng shui will know that this plant is a symbol denoting wealth and the enjoyment of life—what better reason do you need to grow it? But if you're looking for a low-growing companion for tall succulents, then *C. socialis*, also from South Africa, may do the trick. It makes a spreading mat of fleshy, compact, tufted rosettes barely 4 in (10 cm) high, and produces white flowers in spring. Give it a winter minimum of 43–45°F (6–7°C) and plenty of light in both winter and summer.

C. socialis

MORE FOR YOUR MONEY Cuttings root easily at any time of year. Plant a 2–4-in (5–10-cm) section of stem in moist potting mix, place in a well-lit place out of direct sun, and keep just moist.

HOW MUCH LIGHT
Good light conditions are important, especially in winter, and a few hours of direct sunlight are beneficial.

ROOM TEMPERATURE
Happy at 64–75°F (18–24°C). Keep cool in winter when light levels are low to avoid spindly growth.

WHEN TO WATER
During summer, allow potting mix to become partly dry before watering, then moisten thoroughly. Do not allow the pot to stand in a saucer of water. In winter, the potting mix should be kept just moist enough to prevent leaves from shriveling.

SURVIVAL STRATEGY
Though not quite indestructible, this plant tolerates a good deal of neglect. Overwatering is its main enemy. Wipe dust from the leaves occasionally to enjoy their shiny surface. If necessary, pinch out the shoot tips to encourage branching.

SIZE
10 in/25 cm

SITE
South-facing windowsill

Echeveria 'Duchess of Nuremberg', *p.79*

REGULAR, REPEATED PATTERNS create a sense of calm and reassurance, which need not be at the expense of style. With careful choice of plant, pot, and position, you can make bold statements that are easy both to live with and to maintain. Strong shapes work best with simple pots, and the greater the number of repeated elements, the more powerful and dramatic the effect.

Zamioculcas zamiifolia, **p.171**

Sansevieria trifasciata var. *laurentii*, **p.147**

Nephrolepis exaltata 'Bostoniensis', **p.120**

Ctenanthe oppenheimiana 'Tricolor'

Never-never plant

The name *Ctenanthe* comes from the Greek *kteis*, meaning "comb," and *anthos*, "flower," and refers to the arrangement of the bracts. It also gives a clue as to how to say the name; you pronounce both the "c" and the "t." Despite the complicated label, it is an exciting foliage plant that eventually makes a bushy shape around 3 ft (1 m) tall. The long, spear-shaped leaves are streaked with cream and green on their upper surfaces, with pink suffusing through from the rich red-purple undersides. For the most dramatic effect, position it so you can see the backs of the leaves and their shadows on the wall.

C. burle-marxii

HOW MUCH LIGHT
Provide bright filtered light during summer and as much light as possible in winter.

ROOM TEMPERATURE
Normal room temperatures, 64–75°F (18–24°C), are all it asks for. Takes a dip to 50–54°F (10–12°C) in winter.

WHEN TO WATER
Water freely during summer, keeping potting mix moist, but allow it to dry out in winter; this is especially important if the temperature falls to 50–54°F (10–12°C), since wet soil may cause root rot. If the leaves roll up, it means that the plant is too dry.

SURVIVAL STRATEGY
A straightforward plant with no extreme requirements. Fertilize every two weeks when in active growth, but avoid fertilizing during winter. Benefits from extra humidity; mist or stand on a tray of damp pebbles to help prevent leaves from curling in hot conditions.

SIZE
37 in/92 cm

SITE
Bright living room

Cuphea ignea 'Variegata'
Cigar flower

A charming, easily grown, small twiggy plant with rich green, variegated leaves. It has a long season—spring to fall—of narrow, tubular red flowers, each tipped with a speck of purple and white "cigar ash": hence the common name. Give it a place in the sun where it can develop its rounded, bushy shape and show off a mass of tiny flowers. It can reach 24 in (60 cm) high and wide but is better trimmed back in spring to keep it bushy and within bounds. It looks rather poor after a cold winter but soon develops into a showy, colorful plant in spring.

HOW MUCH LIGHT
Cupheas thrive in bright light and full sun.

ROOM TEMPERATURE
Tolerates near-freezing temperatures in winter, but extreme cold can cause leaf drop; 46–50°F (8–10°C) is safer.

WHEN TO WATER
Let it dry out slightly between waterings. Plants allowed to become completely dry will lose their leaves but if watered in time will recover and put out a new set of leaves.

SURVIVAL STRATEGY
Feed every two weeks with a balanced liquid fertilizer. In spring, it can be cut back by half to maintain a nice, full shape and encourage new flowering shoots.

SIZE
13 in/33 cm

SITE
Sunny windowsill

Curcuma alismatifolia
Siam tulip

Curcuma alismatifolia is a very exotic-looking
member of the ginger family from Thailand.
Though pink is the color usually offered,
deep purple and white varieties
are available. The flowers may last
up to three months if kept cool. It
is not the most straightforward plant
to grow if you want to keep it from year
to year because it loses its leaves and becomes
dormant in late fall and stays so until spring;
during this period the rhizome must be kept dry.
However, its showy flowers and the chance to grow
an ever-larger plant each year make it worth trying.
It can, of course, be treated as a short-term plant
and discarded once the flowers have faded.

Striking bracts emerge in summer.

HOW MUCH LIGHT
Give plenty of bright or direct light
for flowers and sturdy growth. Open
flowers last longer in partial shade.

ROOM TEMPERATURE
Summer temperatures of 64–73°F
(18–23°C) are ideal; tolerates winter
lows of 45°F (7°C) when dormant.

WHEN TO WATER
Keep moist but not wet during the
growing season. Do not allow to
stand in a saucer of water. Keep the
dormant rhizome virtually dry.

SURVIVAL STRATEGY
Plant becomes dormant in late fall
after the flowers have finished.
Gradually dry off the roots and
remove the faded foliage. In spring,
repot and move into a warm
environment to stimulate growth.
Benefits from medium to high
humidity.

SIZE

38 in/95 cm

SITE

Bright
contemporary
interior

Cycas revoluta

Japanese sago palm

This is a curious, slow-growing Japanese plant, with a primitive air about it that makes you feel it has changed little over the last few million years. The dark green foliage has a soft, fernlike appearance but is in fact stiff and hard. The leathery leaves arise in an open rosette from what looks like a small, brown, flock-covered pineapple. Mature plants can be 6 ft (2 m) tall, but it grows so slowly that if you buy a 12-in (30-cm) plant to keep indoors, it is never likely to outgrow its allotted space. It needs good light, so is best grown in a conservatory. Though neither a fern or a palm, it associates well with both of these plant types.

HOW MUCH LIGHT
Good, bright light is important if you want it to produce new leaves and not just sit there looking dormant.

ROOM TEMPERATURE
Happily grows at anywhere between 45° and 64°F (7–18°C); even tolerates a few degrees of frost if kept dry.

WHEN TO WATER
At normal room temperature, keep potting mix moist but not water-logged. Reduce watering when winter temperatures are low. Apply a half-strength balanced liquid fertilizer every 2 weeks from spring to late summer.

SURVIVAL STRATEGY
Takes low temperatures, irregular watering, and dry atmospheres in stride, but warmer temperatures, regular watering and fertilizing, and plenty of light will give you a healthier plant that will produce new leaves. In temperate climates, you can put it outdoors for the summer.

SIZE
24 in/60 cm

SITE
Conservatory

Cyclamen persicum
Cyclamen

A popular winter-flowering plant that has not only very showy flowers but also large, attractive leaves marked with silver. Flowers range from scarlet, through pink, to white, some with streaks and others with colored edges. Their petals can be twisted or may have frilly edges. Some are scented, and new varieties are produced regularly. Smaller-flowered cultivars have a charm that is sometimes lacking in the large-flowered hybrids; group several of them together in a single pot to create a colorful display. White cyclamen work well with ferns such as *Pteris argyraea* and *Nephrolepis*.

STOP THE ROT Remove spent flowers and yellowing leaves with their stems intact to prevent decaying stalks from rotting the tuber, especially if the stems are densely crowded.

HOW MUCH LIGHT
Plants in bloom should be given full winter light.

ROOM TEMPERATURE
Cyclamen enjoy cool conditions and will flower longer at temperatures around 55–64°F (13–18°C).

WHEN TO WATER
Wait until the leaves just start to wilt before watering. Always water by standing in a deep saucer of water for 10 minutes, then allow to drain.

SURVIVAL STRATEGY
Feed every 3 weeks with a balanced liquid fertilizer. After flowering, discard, or gradually reduce watering until leaves yellow, then stop watering. In late summer or early fall, clean off and repot tuber. Keep in a bright place with soil just moist until growth starts, then water as normal.

SIZE
14 in/35 cm

SITE
Bedroom, or any bright room

Cymbidium

Cymbidium hybrids

The easiest orchids to grow in the home. There are many hybrids, but plants are often sold with no variety name, relying on their flowers to tempt you into buying them. They vary considerably in height, and flower colors range through pink, white, green, and yellow. All look exotic, and once in flower will last for several weeks.

The labellum (lip) is the most colorful petal.

HOW MUCH LIGHT
Give bright light but avoid scorching sun. Low light levels will discourage flowering.

ROOM TEMPERATURE
Provide a cool winter of 50°F (10°C) for 6–7 weeks, then keep at room temperature (64–75°F/18–24°C).

WHEN TO WATER
These plants resent overwatering, so in winter, be careful to keep them only just moist. In summer, give water when the top of the potting mix has dried out. When misting the leaves, avoid spraying the flowers: they mark easily, and if they remain wet are prone to rotting.

SURVIVAL STRATEGY
Cymbidiums enjoy high humidity; stand on trays of damp pebbles and mist regularly. Use special fertilizers for plants in flower, and for ones in leafy growth. In mild areas you can move them outside for summer to sheltered sites, where they benefit from fresh air and good light levels.

SIZE
26 in/65 cm

SITE
Bright living room

Cyperus involucratus syn. *C. alternifolius*

Umbrella plant

How many houseplants have you killed
by overwatering? Well, perhaps you
should try the umbrella plant,
which actually likes being wet at
the roots. The common name has
nothing to do with its affinity for water
but everything to do with the umbrella-
like arrangement of the flower heads.
The tall, triangular stems are topped
by a starlike head of what look like
leaves but are in fact bracts associated
with the grasslike flowers. Grown
well, it is a very stylish plant: make
the most of its architectural shape
and elegance, and enjoy the
dramatic shadows cast when
it's properly lit.

SPARE UMBRELLAS Shoot tops readily provide
roots and new young plants will quickly form when
they are upturned in a saucer of water. Plant in
moist potting mix when the roots have formed.

HOW MUCH LIGHT
Give it a well-lit position with some
direct sunlight, but avoid placing it
in scorching midday sun.

ROOM TEMPERATURE
Normal room temperatures, 64–75°F
(18–24°C), are sufficient, with a
winter minimum of 45°F (7°C).

WHEN TO WATER
Make sure the roots are continually
moist. To keep up with the large
amounts of water required by
mature plants in summer, create a
water reservoir by standing the pot
in a shallow saucer so that it always
has a drink on tap (see p.105).

SURVIVAL STRATEGY
Provide a balanced liquid fertilizer in
summer when the plant is actively
growing. Plants in direct light will
need high levels of humidity to
prevent leaf tips from going brown.

SIZE
16 in/40 cm

SITE
Bright
living room

Cyrtomium falcatum

Japanese holly fern

The robust, leathery nature of the leaves gives this fern a very unfernlike character, but hints at its considerable toughness compared to its flimsy indoor cousins. The holly-like foliage is unique: use it to add diversity to groups of ctenanthes, davallias, and aspidistras, or among orchids, where its pointed leaves will provide a contrast with their rather ordinary foliage.

HOW MUCH LIGHT
Provide bright light but keep out of hot direct sunshine.

ROOM TEMPERATURE
Normal levels of 64–75°F (18–24°C) are sufficient; unconcerned by near-freezing temperatures in winter.

WHEN TO WATER
Keep potting mix moist throughout the growing season, but allow it to dry out slightly between waterings during winter.

SURVIVAL STRATEGY
Very few requirements if you meet its needs for good light and water. Provide a balanced liquid fertilizer every 3 weeks.

SIZE
14 in/35 cm

SITE
Cool, bright hallway

Davallia canariensis

Hare's-foot fern

It is often assumed that all ferns are filmy, moisture-loving plants, but here is a tough one that withstands occasional drought and grows in conditions of low humidity. It owes its common name to the furry, brown spreading rhizomes. Little bumps on the upper surface of the fronds make it rough to the touch: another unfernlike characteristic. Coming from Spain, it enjoys warmth, yet it stands near-freezing temperatures; it loses its fronds in the cold, but new ones grow when warmer conditions return.

HOW MUCH LIGHT
Give bright light but keep out of direct sunlight.

ROOM TEMPERATURE
Normal room temperature, 64–75°F (18–24°C), is ideal but it tolerates lower temperatures during winter.

WHEN TO WATER
Water regularly but allow the potting mix to dry out partially before the next watering. If temperatures are low, reduce watering and provide just enough water to prevent the soil from drying out completely.

SURVIVAL STRATEGY
Provide plants in active growth with a balanced liquid fertilizer every two weeks. Its tolerance of cool conditions means you can use it to complement flowering plants such as cyclamen or camellia.

SIZE
14 in/35 cm

SITE
Shady kitchen

Dendrobium 'Emma Type'
Orchid

There are dozens of dendrobium species, from which dozens of hybrids have been produced, with flower colors ranging from rich yellows, through lime greens, to pinks and purples. Some have solid-looking flowers, while others are wispy and narrow-petaled. But all are exciting, and as a bonus, *D. nobile,* along with some of its hybrids, is sweetly scented. The good news is that these orchids enjoy cooler temperatures and do not require tropical heat, but good humidity is important.

D. nobile

HOW MUCH LIGHT
Bright filtered light is ideal all year.

ROOM TEMPERATURE
Summer temperatures of around 68–75°F (20–24°C) are adequate, with a winter minimum of 50°F (10°C).

WHEN TO WATER
During the summer months, water weekly by dipping the roots into a container of soft water for 5 minutes then letting it drain thoroughly (see p.181). Keep moisture off the leaves to prevent rot. Dendrobiums should be kept almost dry in winter.

SURVIVAL STRATEGY
A cool winter period encourages flower production, as will providing good winter light. Top-heavy flower stems may need supporting with a cane. Give special orchid fertilizer at every other watering. Provide good humidity—they dislike dry air, particularly at higher temperatures.

SIZE
22 in/56 cm

SITE
Bright living room

Dieffenbachia seguine

Dumb cane

Bold markings and fresh green coloring make this lively plant guaranteed to brighten your home. A word of warning: the sap is toxic and can cause swelling and even loss of speech if you get it in your mouth—hence the common name. There are many varieties, all with different markings but equally easy to care for, provided the atmosphere is not too dry. Move them closer to windows in winter so they get as much light as possible during shorter, darker days.

D. seguine 'Saturn'

HOW MUCH LIGHT
Bright filtered light helps maintain leaf color.

ROOM TEMPERATURE
Winter minimum is 61°F (16°C). Avoid hot summer temperatures if you cannot provide high humidity.

WHEN TO WATER
Keep potting mix moist throughout the growing season. Low winter temperatures will check growth and watering can then be reduced; allow the plant to partially dry out before watering.

SURVIVAL STRATEGY
Brown leaf tips may be a sign of insufficient water, or indicate that the atmosphere is too dry. Stand it on a tray of damp pebbles (see p.178). Don't forget, the sap is toxic, so take care how you handle it, particularly when removing old leaves.

SIZE
20 in/50 cm

SITE
Bright hallway

Dizygotheca elegantissima syn. *Schefflera elegantissima*

False aralia

This plant creates a busy effect and can be used as a foil for larger-leaved plants. The long, narrow leaves are a very dark green, which also makes it good to contrast with the lighter-colored foliage of epipremnum or variegated figs (*Ficus*). On its own, it makes a tall, stately specimen, and against a pale plain backdrop the effect of its silhouette can be extremely striking.

HOW MUCH LIGHT
Bright light will keep the growth compact and the leaves a good dark color. Keep out of hot direct sun.

ROOM TEMPERATURE
Normal room temperature, 64–75°F (18–24°C), is sufficient, with a winter minimum of 55°F (13°C).

WHEN TO WATER
This plant is much more tolerant of drying out than it is of overwatering. Allow potting mix to dry out slightly between waterings, and water sparingly in winter. Misting is beneficial, but use soft water to avoid leaving unsightly white marks on the dark foliage.

SURVIVAL STRATEGY
Dizygothecas normally have an upright habit; pinching out the tips will encourage bushier growth.

SIZE
13 in/33 cm

SITE
Minimalist interiors

Display ideas | Group impact

GROUP ARRANGEMENTS look attractive, and can be functional too: a few tall plants can make a flexible living partition to screen off part of a room. Plants also benefit from the higher levels of humidity generated when they are grown close together. And by moving plants with similar needs into a single pot, you can prolong the interest of a flowering display after the blooms have gone.

Philodendron erubescens, **pp.134–135;** *Ficus deltoidea,* **pp.86–87;** *Philodendron* 'Cobra'; *Epipremnum aureum* 'Marble Queen', **p.80**

Calathea zebrina, C. picturata, C. louisae, **pp.40–41;** *Dracaena,* **p.76–77**   *Exacum,* **p.83;** *Pilea,* **p.137;** *Hypoestes,* **p.101;** *Saintpaulia,* **p.146**

Dracaena marginata
Madagascar dragon tree

Dracaenas are a useful and reliable group of architectural foliage plants. The tufts of narrow leaves of *D. marginata* are perched elegantly at the top of spindly trunks, and the taller they get, the more elegant they become. Lower leaves are shed as the shoot grows higher. Large specimens should be stood against a plain background to emphasize their shape. *D. fragrans* and its varieties are more substantial but less refined: the broader leaves may have greater presence but their style of presentation is heavy-handed, with usually a single head on a much stockier trunk.

CALLING CARDS Adult vine weevils leave telltale notches in leaf edges. They are nocturnal, so pick them off at night.

HOW MUCH LIGHT
Enjoy bright conditions. *D. fragrans* also tolerates semi-shaded positions without losing its variegation.

ROOM TEMPERATURE
Normal room temperature 64–75°F (18–24°C) is sufficient. Avoid winter dips below 57–59°F (14–15°C).

WHEN TO WATER
Keep the potting mix moist during the growing season, but in winter allow it to dry out partially before watering sparingly.

SURVIVAL STRATEGY
Cutting the top off single-stemmed plants of *D. marginata* will cause side branches to shoot. Do this in late spring. Gently pull off spent lower leaves to keep the plant neat.

SIZE
36 in/90 cm

SITE
Living room

Other varieties

D. fragrans Deremensis Group 'Yellow Stripe'
The margins broaden as the arching leaves
expand to their full length of 16 in (40 cm).

D. marginata 'Tricolor' An "improved" take
on the species with stripes in 3 colors on
arching leaves 12–24 in (30–60 cm) long.

D. fragrans Broad, plain green arching leaves
up to 32 in (80 cm) long emerge from a thick
trunk. If you get flowers, they are fragrant.

◁ *D. fragrans* Deremensis Group 'Lemon
and Lime' Tough foliage for shady or well-lit
conditions, arching out to 24 in (60 cm).

Fatsia japonica

Japanese aralia

A common but useful plant, with the advantage that it tolerates the cool conditions found by front doors and in unheated conservatories in winter. The leaves are large and glossy, and although mature plants may produce heads of white flowers, the majority of plants grown indoors never do. A compact version, *F. japonica* 'Moseri', is also worth a try.

F. japonica 'Variegata'

☁ HOW MUCH LIGHT
Grow in bright light for compact growth and dark green leaves.

🌡 ROOM TEMPERATURE
Keep cool: temperatures as low as 36–37°F (2–3°C) in winter will result in compact, healthy-looking plants.

💧 WHEN TO WATER
Water regularly in summer but reduce watering during winter. Wilting leaves will soon tell you that it is ready for a drink. Regular applications of foliar fertilizer will keep the plant's leaves dark green.

✋ SURVIVAL STRATEGY
Clean the leaves with a damp cloth. Do not be afraid to cut back stems of plants that get too tall. Prune them in spring and new sideshoots will soon form to make a bushier plant. Be aware that combinations of high temperatures and low light levels lead to straggly, drawn growth.

SIZE
22 in/56 cm

🏠 SITE
Bright hallway

Ferocactus latispinus

Devil's tongue

There is not much sitting on the fence when it comes to the barrel cactus: either you love their dumpy, leafless growth, furrowed stems, and array of tough, curled, and often colorful spines, or you look at them and wonder what all the fuss is about. With *F. latispinus*, the devil is definitely in the detail. Each bristly set is made up of ten or twelve small whitish spines and four big, red, extremely tough ones, of which the lowest, and largest, curls back. The whole plant is an untouchable delight of texture, shape, and subtle color with—if you are lucky and conditions are ideal—a purple, red, or yellow flower or two.

Prominent curved bristles resemble fishhooks.

☀ HOW MUCH LIGHT
Light is the all-important factor. Provide as much direct sunlight as possible, even in winter.

🌡 ROOM TEMPERATURE
Normal to high room temperatures are ideal, combined with good light. Winter minimum is 45°F (7°C).

✍ WHEN TO WATER
Water regularly in summer, but do not keep the potting mix permanently wet and allow it to dry out between waterings. Keep dry during winter. Benefits from a monthly balanced liquid fertilizer during the warm summer period.

✋ SURVIVAL STRATEGY
Place it outdoors once the danger of frost has passed if it means it will get more light. Use a paintbrush to keep the plant clean, or blow off dust with a drinking straw or a vacuum cleaner adjusted to low suction.

SIZE
8 in/20 cm

🏠 SITE
South-facing windowsill

Ficus elastica
Rubber plant

The fig family provides some excellent plants for the home. In their native habitat many make huge trees, but in the confines of a pot they stay small and manageable— although they make impressive specimens if you have the space and want them big. Rubber plant (*F. elastica*) and weeping fig (*F. benjamina*) are well known and reliable favorites, and rightly so: they are particularly good at removing harmful pollutants from the air. *F. benjamina* is naturally bushy, but to get *F. elastica* to branch out, you need to cut off the growing point when it is small. Do not worry about the white sap that flows out of the cut; it will stop eventually and causes the plant no harm.

F. elastica 'Belgica'

HOW MUCH LIGHT
Often consigned to shady conditions, but figs are healthier in good light, especially the variegated forms.

ROOM TEMPERATURE
All are satisfied with normal room temperature (64–75°F/18–24°C).

WHEN TO WATER
Figs with leathery leaves tolerate being dry better than being too wet. Let the potting mix become partially dry before watering. Overwatering causes leaf drop. *F. pumila* has thinner leaves and should not be allowed to dry out.

SURVIVAL STRATEGY
Figs adapt well to conditions in the home and are among the easiest plants to grow indoors. Fertilize semiweekly when actively growing. Wipe leaves clean with a damp cloth.

SIZE
24 in/60 cm

SITE
Home office; living room

Other varieties

F. sagittata is a small, bushy trailing plant with narrow, fresh-green leaves and a spreading habit; it grows just 6–8 in (15–20 cm) tall.

F. benjamina 'Starlight' is a form of the bushy weeping fig, which can top 6 ft (2 m). Good light is essential to maintain the variegation.

F. binnendijkii 'Alii' is upright with narrow leaves around 8 in (20 cm) long. It prefers bright light, and grows over 6 ft (2 m) tall.

◁ *F. deltoidea* (Mistletoe fig) Naturally bushy, this is the only ornamental fig likely to bear "figs." Alas, they are inedible. To 6 ft (2 m).

Epipremnum aureum 'Marble Queen', **p.80**

NOTHING BRINGS THE OUTSIDE IN like climbers or trailers; they include the most natural-looking and vigorous houseplants around. Some need plenty of space, but slender-stemmed plants are useful for tight corners or recesses. Most are decidedly free-willed and scramble where they will, so you'll need to keep pinching out tips and tying in shoots to keep them from taking over your home.

*Bougainvillea glabra 'Alexandra', **p.37**; Stephanotis floribunda, **p.161***

*Hedera helix, **p.95***

*Philodendron 'Cobra' **pp.134–135***

Fittonia verschaffeltii

Nerve plant

This may be a small plant, but it's one with considerable charm. Its oval leaves are prettily veined in white or pink, depending on the variety. The low-growing creeper spreads gradually, but the shoots root as they go, which means it is easy to propagate. A wide, shallow pot of several plants makes a more appealing display than a single, lone fittonia. It is a plant of the South American rainforests and therefore requires high humidity and warm temperatures; try it in a bottle garden or a terrarium.

HOW MUCH LIGHT
Give bright filtered light but keep out of direct sunlight.

ROOM TEMPERATURE
Try to maintain a year-round temperature of 64°F (18°C), along with good humidity.

WHEN TO WATER
Beware of overwatering fittonias, particularly in winter, since the stems may rot. In summer, keep the potting mix moist but not wet.

SURVIVAL STRATEGY
Warmth and high humidity are essential. Provide a half-strength balanced liquid fertilizer during the summer months when the plant is in full growth.

SIZE
8 in/20 cm

SITE
Bathroom

Gardenia augusta

Gardenia

Gardenias are well-known for their flowers and dark, leathery, evergreen foliage. Growing one is not difficult; getting it to flower again is a different matter. Stable temperatures and humidity are crucial. Sudden temperature changes, drafts, or fluctuating humidity may cause bud drop, as can changing the angle of its light source. Given the fussy demands, you may decide to enjoy it while the flowers last, then buy another plant next year.

Pure white flowers are deliciously scented.

HOW MUCH LIGHT
Position in good bright light but out of direct scorching sun.

ROOM TEMPERATURE
To encourage flowers, provide high humidity and 64–70°F (18–21°C) by day and 61–63°F (16–17°C) at night.

WHEN TO WATER
Use soft water to prevent the leaves from yellowing. Keep the potting mix moist but not wet during summer; reduce watering during the darker winter months. In summer, give it a liquid fertilizer specifically formulated for acid-loving plants.

SURVIVAL STRATEGY
Grow in nonalkaline potting mix, and provide stable temperatures and humidity. For flowers, provide night temperatures below 64°F (18°C); day temperatures must be no higher than 72°F (22°C). Avoid drafts, or moving the plant so that it is at a different angle to its light source.

SIZE
14 in/35 cm

SITE

Living room

Graptopetalum bellum

Graptopetalum

This small, tightly packed succulent punches way above its weight when it comes to flowering. The fleshy leaves form a tight, mounded rosette that rarely gets above an inch or two high and just a few inches across, but the flowers are large, bright, and eye-catching. As long as the plant has plenty of light, the deep pink-red flowers are freely produced, and once in flower the show lasts for several weeks. When not in flower, it can look a little lost if it's grown on its own, so put several together in a wide, shallow pot.

Star-shaped flowers

HOW MUCH LIGHT
Provide as much direct sunlight as possible throughout the year.

ROOM TEMPERATURE
Normal temperatures are sufficient. Cool winters will help to keep it compact when light levels are low.

WHEN TO WATER
From spring to early fall, when the plant is actively growing, water regularly but let the potting mix dry out slightly between waterings. In winter, give just enough water to prevent the soil from drying out completely.

SURVIVAL STRATEGY
Overwatering, particularly during winter, causes root rot. Check to see that the plant is not standing in water inside its cachepot.

SIZE
9 in/23 cm

SITE
South-facing window

Grevillea robusta
Silk oak

If you like plants that get a move on, and you do not mind them on the large size, then this is the one for you. In its native Australia it reaches 50 ft (15 m) or more, but it can certainly be contained in the home for a few years before it outgrows its space. Its fine leaves and graceful habit make it a very attractive foliage plant. It is particularly effective among larger, heavier leaves like those of philodendron or the Swiss cheese plant (*Monstera*). Be prepared to start again after a few years with a new, smaller plant.

HOW MUCH LIGHT
Provide bright light, even full sun. Good light is essential, so move it to the sunniest spot in winter.

ROOM TEMPERATURE
Ordinary room temperature, 64–75°F (18–24°C), is sufficient, with a winter minimum of around 41°F (5°C).

WHEN TO WATER
Use soft water. When the plant is actively growing, water regularly, keeping the potting mix moist but not wet. When growth is slower in winter, allow soil to dry out slightly before watering.

SURVIVAL STRATEGY
Use an ericaceous (nonalkaline) potting mix when potting this fast-growing plant. Provide a liquid fertilizer formulated for acid-loving plants every two weeks throughout the summer growing season.

SIZE
38 in/95 cm

SITE
Conservatory

Gynura aurantiaca
Purple velvet plant

This looks like the kind of plant you might come across if you were to land on an alien planet. The combination of its covering of purple hairs, the toothed and curled leaves, and its smelly orange winter flowers (pinch them off if you cannot bear their aroma) give it an outrageous character that I find irresistible. It starts off upright, but eventually grows sideways and trails out of the pot.

Purple hairs on leaves provide the velvety texture.

🌤 HOW MUCH LIGHT
For the best color, grow this plant in good, bright light.

🌡 ROOM TEMPERATURE
Normal temperatures are sufficient with moderate humidity. The winter minimum is 54–55°F (12–13°C).

💧 WHEN TO WATER
Avoid getting water on the leaves. Keep the potting mix just moist during summer, but reduce watering in winter when temperatures drop.

✋ SURVIVAL STRATEGY
An easy-to-please plant. It will root from pieces of broken-off stem placed in water. You can keep plants compact by pinching out stems, but its trailing habit accounts for a big part of its character, so not too much pruning, please.

📏 SIZE
8 in/20 cm

🏠 SITE
East- or west-facing window

Hedera helix 'Lightfinger'

English ivy

Ivies offer an almost limitless choice of leaf shapes and sizes, and although color is limited to greens, yellows, and whites, there's going to be at least one to suit your taste. There are ivies that climb, ivies that trail, and ivies that make bushy shrubs; all thrive in bathroom, bedroom, or living room as long as they get some light and are watered occasionally. More lavish treatment results in healthier, robust plants.

'White Wonder'

'Pink 'n' Curly'

'Gilded Hawke'

'Kolibri'

☀ HOW MUCH LIGHT
Variegated forms benefit from bright light; plain varieties tolerate shade but are more compact in good light.

🌡 ROOM TEMPERATURE
Too much heat results in straggly, drawn growth. Grow in conditions as cool as possible all year.

💧 WHEN TO WATER
Keep moist in summer and do not allow plants to dry out during winter or their leaves will shrivel up.

✋ SURVIVAL STRATEGY
These are very easy plants to grow. A major plus is that they are both shade- and cold-tolerant, making them ideal for a drafty hallway or an unheated conservatory.

📏 SIZE
11 in/29 cm

🏠 SITE
Bedroom; bathroom

Hemigraphis 'Exotica'

Purple waffle plant

A low-growing compact evergreen with rounded, crinkly leaves that are deeply corrugated and puckered. The foliage is flushed with dark red and purple, almost to the point of appearing black. It bears white flowers from spring to summer that stand out well against the dark leaves. It is not the showiest plant, but it has understated class and is great as groundcover for plants in large pots. Alternatively, use a few individuals as a unifying feature in several group displays. Its compact habit makes it useful for a narrow windowsill or as a filler among larger plants.

HOW MUCH LIGHT
Bright light encourages good leaf color and flowering. Keep out of scorching sun.

ROOM TEMPERATURE
Normal room temperature, 64–75°F (18–24°C). Do not allow it to fall below 54–55°F (12–13°C) in winter.

WHEN TO WATER
Water regularly during the summer months when the plant is in active growth. Reduce watering in winter but do not allow it to become dry.

SURVIVAL STRATEGY
Hemigraphis enjoys the humidity of a microenvironment created by surrounding plants. The higher the temperature, the greater the need for humidity.

SIZE
12 in/30 cm

SITE
Bright windowsill

Hibiscus rosa-sinensis 'Athene'

Rose of China

A very leafy and bushy plant with flamboyant flowers in a wide range of colors—red, white, orange, pink, and yellow. The main flowering season is during summer, but given warm temperatures and good light, flowers may appear on and off year-round. Even when not in flower, the branching habit and dark green leaves make an attractive addition to the general greenery in the house. Give it pride of place, cherish it, and you will be well rewarded.

H. rosa-sinensis

HOW MUCH LIGHT
Plenty of bright light but not midday summer sun. In winter, give it full sun, but keep it moist at the roots.

ROOM TEMPERATURE
Normal temperature is sufficient. Stifling conservatory heat without humidity causes flowers to fade fast.

WHEN TO WATER
Large plants will need regular watering during summer; keep the potting mix moist. In winter, reduce watering and allow the soil to dry out slightly before the next watering.

SURVIVAL STRATEGY
Given a large pot and enough space, specimens can grow to 6 ft (2 m) or more, but if you prune back hard in spring you can keep them within bounds. This does not affect flowering. High-potash fertilizer in early summer encourages flowering.

SIZE
20 in/50 cm

SITE
Airy conservatory

Hippeastrum cultivars

Amaryllis

Hippeastrums manage to combine, on the same plant, some of the most flamboyant flowers with some of the plainest and least interesting leaves. That said, you can certainly overlook its foliage failings when it is in full, overwhelming bloom. Colors of the large trumpet flowers can be anything from blood red to pure white or pale green, and each head can carry as many as five blooms. Make the most of their architectural qualities and distract from their gaunt foliage by growing them in a regimental line in a long trough or as repeated patterns in a row of identical pots.

Open trumpets reveal pollen-laden anthers.

HOW MUCH LIGHT
When in leaf, provide plenty of light, including some direct sun. Too little, and plants are unlikely to flower.

ROOM TEMPERATURE
Will flower at normal temperatures (64–75°F/18–24°C); keep cool when in bloom to prolong the display.

WHEN TO WATER
Dry bulbs should be potted and kept just moist until roots develop and start to take up water; thereafter, keep soil moist at all times in active growth. In late summer, stop watering and let the bulb dry off and the leaves wither. Start watering again in fall to bring it into growth.

SURVIVAL STRATEGY
Getting flowers for second time takes a little care. After flowering, when leaves appear, fertilize and water regularly and give good light. Allow for a dormant period in late summer, and in fall bring back into growth. When actively growing, repot into fresh mix in the same pot.

SIZE
29 in/74 cm

SITE
Minimalist interior

Howea belmoreana

Sentry palm

An upright and potentially large palm (6 ft/2 m plus) with the major advantage that it is tough and tolerates less-than-ideal conditions. It grows in low humidity and will tolerate low light levels—but do not expect it to grow in the dark. Although howeas will suffer difficult conditions, if it can be given good light with reasonable humidity, then it will respond with greater vigor and develop into a healthier and more handsome plant. Elegant, deeply cut, arching fronds on stiff upright stems makes it ideal for standing at the back of a group of shorter plants. Use it to throw shapely shadows across plain walls.

HOW MUCH LIGHT
Enjoys well-lit sites but copes with medium light. Move near windows to maximize low winter light levels.

ROOM TEMPERATURE
Give a winter minimum of 55–57°F (13–14°C), otherwise keep at room temperature 64–75°F (18–24°C).

WHEN TO WATER
Keep potting mix moist during the growing season. Reduce watering in winter and give just enough to prevent the soil from drying out completely. Apply a balanced liquid fertilizer semiweekly in the growing season; stop fertilizing in winter.

SURVIVAL STRATEGY
This is an amenable plant that needs little extra attention as long as it is fertilized and watered. Wipe dust off the leaves with a damp cloth or sponge; it is a time-consuming but—when you see the results—satisfying job.

SIZE
34 in/85 cm

SITE
Bright south-facing living room

Hoya lanceolata subsp. *bella*
Wax flower

There are several hoya species available to the indoor gardener, but of them all, this is the most manageable and compact. Often sold as just *Hoya bella*, this succulent trailing plant with diamond-shaped leaves has clusters of sweetly scented white flowers, each with a purple center. In summer you'll find between eight and ten quite large flowers at the end of each branch. A hanging basket will place the flowers at just the right height for you to appreciate their strong fragrance.

Clusters of summer flowers are sweetly scented.

HOW MUCH LIGHT
To ensure good flowering, give plenty of light. This can be direct sunlight, but not scorching midday sun.

ROOM TEMPERATURE
Normal room temperature, 64–75°F (18–24°C), is suitable all year.

WHEN TO WATER
Water regularly in summer. Reduce watering during winter when the plant is not growing. Apply a half-strength balanced liquid fertilizer every two weeks.

SURVIVAL STRATEGY
Grow in an open potting mix, like that used for orchids. Related *Hoya carnosa* will reach 12–15 ft (4–5 m) in height but can be looped in a circle or wrapped around a frame to keep it within bounds.

SIZE
22 in/55 cm

SITE
Well lit table top

Hypoestes phyllostachya 'Ruby'

Polka-dot plant

If you have ever hastily painted your walls using a roller before covering all your furniture, you will have some idea of the speckled nature of this plant. Each heart-shaped leaf of this small shrubby plant is covered in pink dots. Varieties with larger markings and some with purple, white, or red splashes on the leaves are available. They are fun plants, and a collection of all the varieties in a single pot or grouped together provides useful color year-round.

'Rose'

'White'

HOW MUCH LIGHT
For the best colors, keep in bright light but out of hot direct summer sun. Tolerates direct sun in winter.

ROOM TEMPERATURE
Keep warm. A year-round constant of 64°F (18°C) is ideal. Long periods below 52°F (11°C) cause leaf drop.

WHEN TO WATER
Give ample water during summer, but allow the soil surface to dry between waterings. Water less in winter, and beware of overwatering. It will enjoy a humid atmosphere.

SURVIVAL STRATEGY
The plant has a tendency to become leggy and open over time, so during spring or summer, trim back and pinch out the growing tips to encourage bushiness. Provide a balanced liquid fertilizer in summer; stop fertilizing in the winter months.

SIZE
8 in/20 cm

SITE
Bathroom; living room

Ficus benjamina, **pp.86–87**

PLANTS PROVIDE THE OXYGEN WE BREATHE: no plants, no life. Many also prove their worth as great filters of volatile household pollutants, including formaldehyde, ammonia, and benzene, given off by upholstery, paints, and domestic motors. Choose plants that absorb these chemicals for bedrooms, living rooms, and offices, to make your indoor environment fresher and safer.

Chlorophytum comosum 'Vittatum', **p.52**

Calathea makoyana, **pp.40–41**

Spathiphyllum wallisii, **p.160**

Kalanchoe pumila

Kalanchoe

There is a startling range of kalanchoes, with plenty of shapes, styles, and colors to choose from. *K. pumila* has neat gray-green serrated leaves perfectly complemented by its purple-pink flowers, but the succulent foliage of *K. tomentosa* offers something completely different, with its silver hairs tinted brown at the leaf edges. Such variety means kalanchoes will appeal to anyone of a botanical bent wanting to start a collection. Despite appearances, their cultural needs are not so wildly different that you cannot grow them all in the same conditions.

Pink, urn-shaped flowers appear in spring.

HOW MUCH LIGHT
Plenty of good light: all stand some direct sunlight—the grayer or hairier they are, the more sun they need.

ROOM TEMPERATURE
Normal room temperature; tolerate cooler winter levels as long they do not drop much below 50°F (10°C).

WHEN TO WATER
Kalanchoes are best kept on the dry side and watered from the bottom. Allow the potting mix to partially dry out between waterings, and water sparingly in winter. *K. blossfeldiana* in particular will suffer when over-watered—getting the heart of the plant wet will cause rot.

SURVIVAL STRATEGY
Avoid overwatering. Remove spent flowers on *K. blossfeldiana* to stop flower heads from falling into the heart of the plant and rotting. Feed *K. blossfeldiana* every two weeks with a balanced liquid fertilizer. Other kalanchoes may be fed monthly.

SIZE
18 in/45 cm

SITE
Bathroom

K. blossfeldiana 'Calandiva' (Flaming Katy)
The tight clusters of sophisticated rosebud
flowers on this plant grow to 12 in (30 cm).

K. mangini hybrids have the largest blooms,
and a long flowering season. Their open,
branching stems reach 10–12 in (25–30 cm).

K. blossfeldiana (Flaming Katy) hybrids come
in bright reds and pastels. Flowers last up to
12 weeks, but plants may not bloom again.

◁ *K. tomentosa* is an irresistible tactile delight.
The brown edge fades as leaves mature but is
prolonged by full sun. Grows to 3 ft (1 m).

Lotus maculatus
Parrot's beak

This is a native of the Canary Islands and a very showy plant when hung with dozens of its vibrant parrot's-bill flowers. When not in flower, it makes a stylish tangle of trailing, frizzy gray foliage. Use it in a basket or let it dangle from a shelf; a well-grown plant will trail 28–32 in (70–80 cm). Flowers come in waves with the main flush in early summer.
L. berthelotti is a red-flowered lookalike.

HOW MUCH LIGHT
Provide as much light as possible throughout the year; it will tolerate full direct sun.

ROOM TEMPERATURE
Best at normal room temperature, 64–75°F (18–24°C), all year, but takes winter lows of 41–43°F (5–6°C).

WHEN TO WATER
Make sure it stays moist throughout the growing season. Keep it on the dry side when temperatures are low in winter.

SURVIVAL STRATEGY
Regular fertilizing will encourage flowering. Cut back straggly growth at any time of the year. Ensure that it gets good light during winter.

SIZE
10 in/25 cm

SITE
Hanging basket

Mandevilla × *amabilis* 'Alice du Pont'

Mandevilla

There are several species of mandevilla, all of which require more or less the same treatment. They are twining climbers: to show them at their best, allow them to meander along a wall on a trellis or wires. Alternatively, keep them quite compact in a pot by pruning back after flowering and wrapping the stems around a frame. *M. laxa* is more cold-tolerant and has scented flowers.

HOW MUCH LIGHT
Good light is needed to encourage flowering. Avoid direct scorching sun but otherwise give plenty of light.

ROOM TEMPERATURE
Normal room temperature, 64–75°F (18–24°C), with a winter minimum of 59–61°F (15–16°C).

WHEN TO WATER
Water regularly in the growing season. Large plants in small pots will need daily checking in warm weather. Water sparingly in winter, but do not allow potting mix to dry out, since the plant needs moisture to sustain its evergreen leaves.

SURVIVAL STRATEGY
Flowers are produced on the current season's growth, so encourage a greater number of new shoots—and therefore more blooms—by cutting back hard after flowering.

SIZE
18 in/45 cm

SITE
Conservatory

Maranta leuconeura var. *erythroneura*
Prayer plant

Marantas are very beautiful foliage plants from the tropical woodland floor. Some of their leaf markings are so neat and precise that they look unreal, especially in this red-veined variety. They have a gradually spreading, low-growing habit, and are ideal for growing around the base of taller plants in wide, shallow pots, where they will enjoy the protection from direct sunlight. Each evening, the leaves roll themselves up and stand erect, hence one of several common names: "prayer plant." The flowers—produced on and off from midsummer to fall—are insignificant and are best removed.

Bright red veins resemble herring bones.

 HOW MUCH LIGHT
Keep in bright, indirect light, and avoid hot sunshine.

 ROOM TEMPERATURE
Maintain a minimum temperature of 61°F (16°C) all year. Match summer heat with higher humidity.

 WHEN TO WATER
Keep moist by watering abundantly in summer. Reduce watering when temperatures are low.

 SURVIVAL STRATEGY
Marantas do not enjoy dry air: the warmer it is, the more humidity they need. Dust and water stains spoil the look of the foliage, so keep them clean using a damp cloth, and be careful to avoid splashing the leaves with water.

 SIZE
31 in/77 cm

 SITE
Shady living room

Monstera deliciosa

Swiss cheese plant

Along with aspidistra, this must be the most mocked and clichéd houseplant of all time. But it is still around, and for my money it is one of the best and easiest foliage plants available. It is naturally a climber, so do not be surprised if its supporting roots start clambering up your walls. It is also a potentially big plant that needs space to be seen at its best— leaves of 24 in (60 cm) or more across are not unknown. Well-grown plants in good light will have deeply lobed leaves perforated with large holes to reduce resistance to high winds—not usually a problem in most homes.

M. deliciosa 'Variegata'

HOW MUCH LIGHT
Good bright light is essential for large healthy leaves, but keep out of direct sun in summer.

ROOM TEMPERATURE
Comfortable room temperature, 64–75°F (18–24°C), with a winter minimum of 50°F (10°C).

WHEN TO WATER
Water regularly during the summer growing season. Reduce watering during winter and be sure not to leave it standing in water. The higher the temperature, the greater need for humidity to prevent the tips of its leaves from browning.

SURVIVAL STRATEGY
Keep the leaves clean with a regular wipe using a damp cloth. In particularly warm weather, spray regularly to raise levels of humidity. Do not be afraid to cut stems back in spring to keep the plant within bounds; sideshoots will soon appear.

SIZE
5 ft/1.5 m

SITE
Large bathroom

Tillandsia cyanea, **p.165**

IF YOU'RE LOOKING TO BRING NATURE INDOORS, where better to start than your bathroom? Hard, tiled surfaces and functional styling cry out for plants to soften them. It's often the most humid room in the house, which suits a range of plants, and it may be brighter than you think; light entering through the smallest window is maximized when it bounces off tiles and mirrors.

Phalaenopsis, **p.133**

Asplenium nidus, **p.31**

Adiantum capillus-veneris, **p.20**

Soleirolia soleirolii, **p.154**

Peperomia caperata hybrids

Peperomia

The rat-tail flower spike is most definitely
the distinguishing feature of all peperomias,
although in a bid for individuality, some
hybrids of *P. caperata* have gone a step farther
and developed flattened tips to
their tails. But their leaves are
bewilderingly different: some
are rounded, juicy, and glossy;
others are deeply crinkled and
glistening. And while most are
crowded and compact, others string
themselves out on scandent stems. All
peperomias are easily grown in lightly
shaded conditions; try combining several in
a single planting to create a rich display of
foliage shapes and colors.

FADING OUT Remove the entire flower
stalks as they fade, in case they drop into
the base of the plant and cause rotting.

☼ **HOW MUCH LIGHT**
Keep out of direct sunlight but give
plenty of bright filtered light.

🌡 **ROOM TEMPERATURE**
Normal temperatures, but they will
not tolerate cold conditions; winter
minimum is 57–59°F (14–15°C).

💧 **WHEN TO WATER**
Peperomias are very susceptible to
overwatering and will quickly rot.
Allow plants to dry out partly before
watering, and then water sparingly,
keeping the heart of the plant dry.
P. caperata will not be harmed if you
let it start to wilt before watering.

✋ **SURVIVAL STRATEGY**
Plants that become too wet are
prone to rotting among their
congested stems, particularly if old
leaves or flowers rest in the crown.
Growing them in terra-cotta pots will
help to keep the plants dry.

📏 **SIZE**
15 in/38 cm

🏠 **SITE**
Bathroom

Other varieties

P. obtusifolia has rounded, glossy leaves and reaches just 10 in (25 cm). Brightly patterned variegated forms are also available.

P. caperata 'Luna Red' forms a compact mound of crinkled leaves with pink-tinged spikes of tiny flowers on dark red stems.

P. rotundifolia makes a mat of rounded leaves and is barely 1 in (3 cm) high. May produce small yellow-green flower spikes in summer.

◁ *P. griseo-argentea* is compact, growing to 16 in (5 cm), with sparkling silver leaves and green "tails" to 3 in (8 cm) high in summer.

Dracaena fragrans Deremensis Group 'Lemon and Lime', **pp.76–77**

AT FIRST SIGHT IT MAY SEEM IMPOSSIBLE to find a plant that will thrive in parts of the house that receive little or no direct light, such as stairwells and hallways. Fortunately, some plants—often those with large, dark, or densely packed leaves—have adapted to life beneath bigger neighbors in the wild, and many of them make excellent subjects for the darker corners of your rooms.

Aspidistra elatior, **p.30**

Adiantum capillus-veneris, **p.20**

Monstera deliciosa, **p.115**

Pericallis × *hybrida* Brilliant Series

Florists' cineraria

A traditional flowering houseplant that should be
treated as a short-lived but showy centerpiece, then
discarded. Buy a plant in bud, keep it cool, and you
will get several weeks of flowering out of it. The
daisylike flowers are brightly colored and range
through pink, blue, red, copper, and white; some
have a white eye and others are solid-colored.

P. × *hybrida* Spring Glory Series

☼ HOW MUCH LIGHT
Good light is important, but keep out
of direct sunlight; cool conditions are
beneficial.

🌡 ROOM TEMPERATURE
Cool temperatures around 57–61°F
(14–16°C) are ideal and will keep
flowers blooming longer.

💧 WHEN TO WATER
Drying out at any time greatly
reduces the length of the flowering
period; keep the potting mix
constantly moist but not too wet.

✋ SURVIVAL STRATEGY
If the demands for moisture and
coolness are met, then this plant
flowers over a long period. No
feeding is necessary, since plants
are discarded. Aphids and whitefly
may be a problem (see p.187).

SIZE
16 in/40 cm

🏠 SITE
Bright
dining
room

Phalaenopsis cultivars
Moth orchid

For elegant sprays of large flowers borne on strong, arching stems up to 36 in (90 cm) long, look no further. There are many hybrids in different shades, including pink, white, and red, with various markings on the flowers, but all need the same growing conditions. Epiphytic (tree-dwelling) orchids, such as this moth orchid, have rambling roots that spread across the surface of the pot and out, searching for nutrients and support. The roots contain chlorophyll and therefore produce energy from light, so growing the plants in open lattice baskets or clear pots is advantageous; you will also see more easily if the roots are wet or dry.

Flowers may appear at any time of year.

HOW MUCH LIGHT
Bright light, but not direct sunlight. Provide plenty of extra artificial light in winter to encourage flowering.

ROOM TEMPERATURE
Ideally about 68°F (20°C), with high humidity. Cool nights are important: allow a dip of around 5–6 degrees.

WHEN TO WATER
Water freely during the growing season. Reduce watering in winter and keep almost dry. Plants benefit from regular spraying with soft water, but avoid spraying their flowers. Do not allow water to sit on the leaves—it may cause rotting, especially in low temperatures.

SURVIVAL STRATEGY
In summer, fertilize semiweekly with orchid fertilizer by dunking roots in the solution for 5 minutes and allowing to drain. After flowering, cut stem back to the 2nd-lowest bud to get a new flowering shoot. Or remove the old stem completely for an even more shapely new shoot.

SIZE
24 in/62 cm

SITE
Bathroom

Philodendron erubescens
Philodendron

Philodendrons are among the most dramatic foliage plants. *P. erubescens* has many varieties, some with rich red leaves and others softly suffused with gold. It is sometimes known as "blushing philodendron," from *erubescens*—the Greek for "red." But the most common—and controllable—philodendron is *P. scandens*, the sweetheart vine, named for its large, heart-shaped leaves, with stems that will root themselves to a moss pole as they climb. Without support, they trail down, providing a swath of rich green foliage. If you want to give a home to the impressive *P. bipinnatifidum,* be sure to give it plenty of space to show its enormous and unusual leaves at their best. Philodendrons are easy plants to grow given just a minimum of care, but look out for scale insects (see p.187).

WATER RESERVES Cut the base off a bottle and prick a tiny hole in the cap to provide enough water for a few days away.

HOW MUCH LIGHT
Keep out of the scorching midday sun but provide good, bright light for healthy, well-colored leaves.

ROOM TEMPERATURE
Normal room temperature, 64–75°F (18–24°C), is adequate, with a winter minimum of 57–59°F (14–15°C).

WHEN TO WATER
When the plant is actively growing, water regularly, keeping the potting mix just moist but not wet. When growth slows in winter, allow the soil to dry out partially before watering sparingly.

SURVIVAL STRATEGY
Keep the leaves clean with a damp cloth to show them at their best. Tie climbing species to a moss pole, keeping the pole moist to encourage the plant's aerial roots to cling. Fertilize regularly during the summer growing season. Cut back vigorous plants at any time.

SIZE
5 ft/1.5 m

SITE
Bathroom

Other varieties

P. bipinnatifidum Sprouts hefty, snakelike aerial roots and dramatic, deeply lobed leaves up to 3 ft (1 m) long from a rather squat trunk.

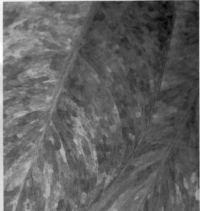

P. domesticum 'Fantasy' Leathery foliage gives this spade-leaved climber, which can reach 20 ft (6 m), some resistance to low humidity.

P. 'Imperial Red' A nonclimbing variety that gradually reaches 3 ft (1 m). The deep red leaves turn greener as they age.

◁ *P. scandens* 'Cobra' Keeps its bold stripes even in shady corners, but benefits from moving closer a the window in winter.

Phoenix canariensis

Canary Island date palm

An easily grown palm that develops a rough, fibrous, rounded base as it matures. The tough leaves are stiff and spiny but beautifully arranged. It's a good conservatory plant, but do not expect to get any dates. It tolerates surprisingly cool conditions, and succeeds at near-freezing temperatures if you keep it dry in winter. *P. roebelenii* is a softer, more delicate plant, and does not stand low temperatures.

☼ HOW MUCH LIGHT
The tough leaves of this plant enjoy bright, direct light. Keep it out of shade and in a well lit position.

🌡 ROOM TEMPERATURE
Although it withstands cold winters, it grows most satisfactorily at room temperature. 64–75°F (18–24°C).

✋ WHEN TO WATER
Water freely during summer when in full growth. Reduce watering in winter, and keep the potting mix only just moist.

✋ SURVIVAL STRATEGY
Regular fertilizing during summer keeps the foliage a good dark green color. The leaves are particularly spiny, and anyone with children should be aware of the danger to their eyes.

▯ SIZE
26 in/65 cm

⌂ SITE
Conservatory

Pilea cadierei
Aluminum plant

Pileas are attractive small foliage plants with very diverse leaf shapes and an array of interesting common names. *P. cadierei*, from Vietnam, has robust corrugated leaves with aluminum-silver markings. *P. involucrata*, the friendship plant, weighs in with strikingly marked, textured foliage. The tiny leaves of the relatively short-lived South American *P. microphylla* give it a fernlike appearance, but it is the flowers that earn it the common name of artillery plant: when mature, they explode, scattering pollen far and wide. All pileas need more or less the same conditions; try them together as a neat foliage group.

P. microphylla

P. involucrata

HOW MUCH LIGHT
Keep out of direct sunlight; partial shade is ideal.

ROOM TEMPERATURE
Avoid high summer temperatures without high humidity; winter minimum is 52–57°F (11–14°C).

WHEN TO WATER
When actively growing, keep the potting mix moist but not wet. At cooler winter temperatures, when the plants are dormant, reduce watering and let the soil become partly dry before watering sparingly.

SURVIVAL STRATEGY
Take care: overwatering is a common problem. Apply a balanced liquid fertilizer every other week during the summer growing season. Old plants may become straggly and, although pinching back the stems can encourage bushiness, they are generally best replaced.

SIZE
7 in/18 cm

SITE
Medium-lit tabletop

Platycerium bifurcatum

Common staghorn fern

This is a curious-looking fern whose common name is distinctly apt. It normally grows up in trees in relatively high humidity and at warm temperatures, so it is slightly demanding in its needs, but when grown well, a large specimen is a striking sight. It bears two types of fronds. One supports the plant on the tree and spreads from the base of the plant and eventually turns brown. The other provides the erect gray-green "leaves."

HOW MUCH LIGHT
It enjoys bright light, but avoid placing it in hot, direct sun without providing high humidity.

ROOM TEMPERATURE
Room temperatures of 64–75°F (18–24°C) are sufficient, with a winter minimum of 55°F (13°C).

WHEN TO WATER
The flat supporting frond tends to spread over the pot, making it almost impossible to check for dryness and difficult to water from the top. Dunk it in a bowl when it shows signs of drooping, and allow to drain. Reduce watering in winter to a quick dip.

SURVIVAL STRATEGY
Give it a half-strength balanced liquid fertilizer every month throughout summer. Stop fertilizing during winter. Regular misting and high humidity will be beneficial. Any dust should be blown off the fronds because attempts to wipe it off will remove the fine covering of down.

SIZE
14 in/35 cm

SITE
Hanging basket

Plumbago auriculata

Cape leadwort

Here is a plant of great charm and lightness. It is a vigorous scrambling plant with light green leaves and open heads of pale blue flowers that are produced throughout the summer. Ideally, it needs the space of a conservatory, where its long shoots can be given some elbow room; otherwise, wrap the shoots around a wire frame or tie them in to a trellis. It flowers on the current season's growth, so prune it back to a framework of mature branches in spring to promote new flowering shoots.

HOW MUCH LIGHT
This plant needs plenty of light and will take full sun as long as it is kept moist at the roots.

ROOM TEMPERATURE
Benefits from winter temperatures of around 50°F (10°C). Provide maximum light for warmer winters.

WHEN TO WATER
Keep the plant moist—but not waterlogged—throughout summer. Keep it dryer during the winter resting period.

SURVIVAL STRATEGY
This is a self-reliant plant that should perform well as long as it is fed regularly with a balanced liquid fertilizer and given plenty of light. Removing the long shoots during summer will reduce flowering, so cut them off in early spring. Check for whitefly occasionally (see p.187).

SIZE
22 in/55 cm

SITE
Conservatory; south-facing window

Pteris cretica 'Alexandrae'
Cretan brake

Pteris are striking and elegant ferns, with their fronds usually held on thin, erect stems, giving the plants an air of elegance and openness. Their requirements are minimal and they make very reliable houseplants. The tall stems and splayed fronds of 'Alexandrae' lend it the appearance—and all the appeal—of a wayward firework. Set it against a light background to show off its shapely silhouette.

Crested tips add an alien touch to the fronds.

☼ HOW MUCH LIGHT
Keep out of direct sun but provide bright filtered light all year.

⏱ ROOM TEMPERATURE
Withstands winter lows of 36–37°F (2–3°C). Keep humidity levels high in hot summer conditions.

♒ WHEN TO WATER
Keep moist throughout the growing season. Reduce watering slightly during periods of low temperature but do not allow it to dry out.

✋ SURVIVAL STRATEGY
Apply a semiweekly dose of balanced liquid fertilizer. In warm temperatures, maintain high humidity by standing the plant on a tray of moist pebbles and misting regularly (see p.178).

▯ SIZE
24 in/60 cm

⌂ SITE
Bathroom

Punica granatum var. *nana*

Dwarf pomegranate

This is a small version of the pomegranate, and although it may produce tiny fruits late in the season, they are really not edible. Its main attraction is its bright orange flowers that are produced over a long period from early summer to fall. It is a deciduous plant; after it has lost its leaves, keep it cool, at around 50°F (10°C). A good plant for the conservatory.

HOW MUCH LIGHT
This is a plant that normally enjoys a Mediterranean climate, so provide maximum light during summer.

ROOM TEMPERATURE
Accepts normal temperatures, 64–75°F (18–24°C), in summer; ideal winter levels are around 50°F (10°C).

WHEN TO WATER
Keep the potting mix moist during the summer. In winter, give just enough water to prevent it from drying out.

SURVIVAL STRATEGY
Feed regularly during summer. Since it has no leaves in winter, and therefore little need for light, you can tuck it away out of sight until growth begins again in spring.

SIZE
16 in/40 cm

SITE
South-facing window

Ananas comosus var. *variegatus*, **p.27**

THE BRIGHT CONDITIONS of a conservatory can be a haven for houseplants; if you provide the right environment, you can create an exotic indoor garden to enjoy all year. Conservatories may get extremely hot if they are not ventilated in summer; few plants tolerate such extremes without being scorched and frizzled, and even drought-tolerant plants need at least some water in the heat.

Dracaena marginata, **pp.76–77**

Passiflora caerulea, **p.126**

Brugmansia candida, **p.38;** *Olea europea,* **p.123;** × *Citrofortunella microcarpa,* **p.55**

Saintpaulia cultivars
African violet

Ask anyone to name three houseplants and the chances are that this will be one of them. African violets seem to have been around since the beginning of time, and the hybridizers have been hard at work ever since, producing varieties with double, frilled, ruffled, and bicolored flowers in pinks, blues, and whites, and pretty well every shade in between. There are also plants with variegated foliage.

'Dorothy'   'Fancy Pants'

'Porcelain'   'Mina'

HOW MUCH LIGHT
Good light is needed for continuous flowering, but avoid direct sunlight.

ROOM TEMPERATURE
Even levels of 63–73°F (17–23°C) are best. Cold drafts and fluctuating temperatures prevent flowering.

WHEN TO WATER
Water from the bottom and allow to drain. The plant's roots are in danger of rotting if the potting mix is kept too wet, so allow it to dry out slightly between waterings. The cooler the temperature, the dryer the soil should be.

SURVIVAL STRATEGY
Rotting in the heart of the plant is always a risk. Do not allow the crown to get wet, and always remove spent flowers. Pull off any damaged foliage but make sure you do not leave any stubs that are likely to rot.

SIZE
8 in/20 cm

SITE
Bright tabletop

Sansevieria trifasciata 'Laurentii'
Mother-in-law's tongue

S. trifasciata is originally from central Africa and closely related to spiky agaves. It is so easy to grow that it has acquired something of a reputation for being dull and uninteresting, and its common name has certainly not helped. Do not be fooled: it's a useful and attractive foliage plant that may even give you flowers if it gets a long, warm summer and good light. And although they are produced erratically, the lax spikes of greenish-white flowers have a sweet nighttime fragrance well worth waiting for. Several variously shaped and colored cultivars have arisen, making it ideal for the enthusiast to start a small, easily cared for collection.

MAKING MORE TONGUES Propagate by easing apart the rootstock and cutting through it with a sharp knife. Plant the offsets in free-draining potting mix and a pot that provides good drainage.

HOW MUCH LIGHT
Enjoys bright light and takes full sun if kept moist. In winter, give as much light as possible.

ROOM TEMPERATURE
Most comfortable at around 64–77°F (18–25°C), but no lower than 52–54°F (11–12°C) in winter.

WHEN TO WATER
Keep potting mix moist, but not wet, when in active growth. During dormancy, keep it almost dry: allow soil to dry out before watering moderately. Do not get water into the heart of the plant. Cold conditions may cause the leaves to rot at the base, particularly if overwatered.

SURVIVAL STRATEGY
Practically indestructible, unless it's overwatered. This is a slow-growing plant and deep shade will make it slower still. Wipe the leaves clean with a damp cloth. Only repot when potbound. Propagate by division or leaf cuttings—but leaf cuttings will lose their variegation.

SIZE

31 in/78 cm

SITE

Minimalist interior

Schefflera arboricola
Umbrella tree

Although slightly more diminutive than the equally common *S. actinophylla*, this umbrella tree displays all the toughness of its big brother. Its leathery foliage, held on umbrella-style stalks, makes it resistant to dry air and even to the occasional drying out. The variegated leaves of this variety lighten the otherwise rather gloomy dark green of its foliage. Its growth is naturally upright: pinch out the shoot tips to keep it bushy. This is a reliable plant that seems to tolerate a degree of neglect.

GOOD GROOMING Keep the foliage clean to get healthier plants; dusty leaves gather less light and so provide less energy. Wipe the leaves clean with a damp cloth, supporting them from below.

HOW MUCH LIGHT
Needs good light conditions, but not direct hot summer sun.

ROOM TEMPERATURE
Normal room temperature, 64–75°F (18–24°C), is sufficient. Warmer conditions require greater humidity.

WHEN TO WATER
Keep moist during the growing season. Reduce watering during winter but do not allow the potting mix to dry out completely.

SURVIVAL STRATEGY
Feed every two weeks with a balanced liquid fertilizer during the growing season. Large, leggy plants can be cut back by half in spring to stimulate bushy sideshoots.

SIZE
18 in/45 cm

SITE
Living room

Schlumbergera hybrids

Christmas cactus

This popular cactus, with spreading foliage and successive, pendulous flowers, is a cross between *S. truncata* and *S. russelliana*. Further hybridizing has led to more colors, including white, orange, and yellow. For good flowering, provide long nights of uninterrupted darkness—which means no artificial light—in fall. Blooms often appear in late winter, so don't panic if you wake up to find there are none open on Christmas Day.

HOW MUCH LIGHT
Keep out of scorching summer sun but give lots of light in winter. If plant is turned, buds may drop (see p.179).

ROOM TEMPERATURE
Normal room temperature, 64–75°F (18–24°C), is ideal all year. Plants in bloom last longer in cooler rooms.

WHEN TO WATER
Use soft water to help maintain slightly acidic conditions. Keep on the dry side for a few weeks after flowering, then water regularly so that potting mix remains moist but is not waterlogged. Provide a high-potash fertilizer every 3–4 weeks in summer.

SURVIVAL STRATEGY
Drafts, overwatering, and cold temperatures can cause buds to drop. Keep hybrids above 59°F (15°C) to hold their color. In temperate climates, plants can be put outside in summer, but keep out of direct sun. Use light, free-draining nonalkaline potting mix.

SIZE
18 in/45 cm

SITE
Hanging basket

Sedum morganianum

Donkey's tail

This is a deliciously chunky succulent with a relaxed attitude
to life, as it lolls out of its pot and hangs in gray, ever-
lengthening dreadlocks that may reach 24–28 in (60–70 cm).
To make the most of its shape, let it drip from a hanging
basket. The gray coating is encouraged by direct sun and gives
the plant its attractive matte finish. Be careful
how you handle it, since the fleshy leaf
segments come off easily when touched.

HOW MUCH LIGHT
Provide full sunlight to ensure
compact growth. Good winter light
is important.

ROOM TEMPERATURE
Normal room temperature. 64–75°F
(18–24°C). Tolerates cooler winters,
but keep above 50°F (10°C).

WHEN TO WATER
During summer, water regularly,
letting the potting mix dry out
slightly between waterings. Never
leave it standing in water. In winter,
reduce watering and let the soil
become almost dry before giving
just a moderate amount of water.

SURVIVAL STRATEGY
This is an easy and straightforward
plant to care for. Give it a balanced
liquid fertilizer every month during
the growing period. The fleshy
leaves are likely to root and develop
into new plants if placed base-down
on the surface of potting mix that is
just moist.

SIZE
12 in/30 cm

SITE
End table

Selaginella martensii 'Watsoniana'

Selaginella

Here is a plant with something of a split personality. It looks like a fern but it isn't one; yet to confuse matters, it produces spores—just like a fern. Despite its identity crisis, it's an easy and fun plant to grow. Its fronds arch out, sending down roots as they spread, which makes it useful for tucking into big pots or among large groups of plants to provide groundcover. It also makes a neat individual specimen for a shady corner.

Feather-like leaves create a fluffy textured effect.

HOW MUCH LIGHT
Selaginella enjoys a semi-shaded position out of direct sunlight.

ROOM TEMPERATURE
Normal levels, 64–75°F (18–24°C), are fine. It likes a humid atmosphere; the leaves will shrivel in hot, dry air.

WHEN TO WATER
Keep the soil moist but not wet. Use soft water. In warm conditions, the plant will grow throughout the year and need constant watering. Where winter temperatures are cooler, watering may be reduced, but never let the potting mix dry out because the leaves will shrivel.

SURVIVAL STRATEGY
This plant suffers in dry conditions, so regular misting with water at room temperature is appreciated. Rooted fronds may be split off to form new plants at almost any time of the year.

SIZE
12 in/30 cm

SITE
Bathroom; kitchen

Senecio macroglossus 'Variegatus'

Cape ivy

If at first glance you mistake this for an ivy, you are forgiven. It climbs or trails just like ivy, but a closer look reveals that, unlike ivy, it has shiny succulent leaves, and—unlike ivy— it climbs by twining its stems around its support. It is a handsome plant with strong variegation that contrasts well with the dark stems. Given a framework to scale, it reaches 28 in (70 cm) or more in height; equally, it will trail down a similar distance if allowed to spill from a shelf or hanging basket. Its cousin, *S. rowleyanus,* is a strikingly different character, with no upwardly mobile aspirations whatsoever: its strings of green beads simply hang vertically from its pot.

S. rowleyanus (String of beads)

⛅ HOW MUCH LIGHT
Both senecios need good light and benefit from some direct sunlight, but not hot, afternoon summer sun.

🌡 ROOM TEMPERATURE
Anywhere between 57° and 72°F (14–22°C) is suitable, with a winter minimum of 50°F (10°C).

💧 WHEN TO WATER
When plants are actively growing— from spring to late summer—water regularly, allowing potting mix to dry slightly before the next watering. Reduce watering during the cooler months and be careful to avoid overwatering.

✋ SURVIVAL STRATEGY
To keep *S. macroglossus* within bounds, either train the stems around a framework or pinch out the shoot tips. *S. rowleyanus* can be left to hang: simply cut off the stems when they are too long. Shoots of both will root easily when tucked into the soil surface.

SIZE
20 in/51 cm

🏠 SITE
Tabletop; hanging basket

Solanum pseudocapsicum

Christmas cherry

A bright and cheerful plant that is at its most interesting when the berries are changing color and it carries a mixed display of green, yellow and orange fruits. It is also a tough plant that will provide winter color for many seasons. The berries may tempt children, but they are toxic and must not be eaten, so keep your plant well out of the reach of young fists. Dwarf varieties reach about 12 in (30 cm) but left alone, the straight species hits 3 ft (1 m) or more in height.

HOW MUCH LIGHT
Enjoys a spell outside in summer, where it will benefit from full light. Keep it out of scorching midday sun.

ROOM TEMPERATURE
No need for heat: happy with normal levels of 64–75°F (18–24°C), and a winter minimum of 50°F (10°C).

WHEN TO WATER
Keep well watered and provide a regular application of balanced liquid fertilizer throughout its life. Reduce watering and stop feeding for several weeks when berries wither in late winter, to give the plant a rest.

SURVIVAL STRATEGY
Regular daily misting when in flower helps ensure a good crop of berries. After the late winter dormant period, cut back by one third, repot, and place outside when the danger of frost has passed. Pinch out growing tips to encourage bushy growth.

SIZE
14 in/36 cm

SITE
Bright table top display

Soleirolia soleirolii 'Aurea'

Baby's tears

This is a tiny and easy plant with a great deal of charm. Its spreading mat or bun of closely-packed leaves is ideal for simple arrangements, or as groundcover in the pots of larger plants and in conservatory beds. You can control its expansive nature by simply cutting it back with scissors, or on large plants by pulling out shoots by hand. 'Aurea' is one of two color variants on the species; the other is 'Variegata', and both are ever ready to revert to plain green, so cut out any reverted shoots right away—a fiddly but necessary job.

S. soleirolii 'Variegata'

S. soleirolii

☁ HOW MUCH LIGHT
Good light will keep plants compact, but avoid direct sun, which is likely to scorch the foliage.

🌡 ROOM TEMPERATURE
Takes 23°F (−5°C): high temperatures will cause it to become leggy. Ideally, keep cool, around 50–61°F (10–16°C).

💧 WHEN TO WATER
Keep the potting mix moist. The foliage will quickly turn brown if it the plant dries out. Higher temperatures demand greater humidity.

✋ SURVIVAL STRATEGY
Beyond making sure it does not dry out, this little plant requires little attention. To make new plants, dig out a small section with a spoon and place it in a pot of fresh potting mix. Kept cool and moist it will soon establish itself and start filling out.

SIZE
7 in/18 cm

🏠 SITE
North-facing windowsill

Solenostemon Wizard Series

Coleus

The old name, *Coleus*, is less of a tongue-twister, and is still widely used. These are among the most startling foliage plants around, and regularly go in and out of fashion. The color range covers red, orange, yellow, every shade of green, pink, copper, and almost black. The shape and patterning of the leaves is almost infinitely varied. There are over a hundred named varieties, but they're usually offered in unnamed mixed selections. Pay your money and take your chance.

S. 'Inky Fingers'

HOW MUCH LIGHT
Despite their sometimes fragile appearance, they tolerate full sun as long as they are moist at the roots.

ROOM TEMPERATURE
Normal temperature, with a winter minimum of 52–54°F (11–12°C). Low temperatures may cause leaf drop.

WHEN TO WATER
These are leafy plants that need a lot of water in warm conditions and should be checked regularly. Keep the potting mix moist. Reduce watering in lower temperatures. Be very careful not to overwater.

SURVIVAL STRATEGY
Feed semiweekly with a balanced liquid fertilizer. Coleus flowers are insignificant and best pinched out before they develop. Pinch out shoot tips, too, to encourage branching and a bushy shape. Summer cuttings root easily in a jar of water.

SIZE
13 in/32 cm

SITE
East- or west-facing window

Display ideas | Chill-proof plants

*Agave attenuata, **p.23***

THERE'S NO ARGUING that plants in porches or hallways provide a friendly, welcoming touch, but often a blast from an open door or drafts through old windows cause them to catch their death. Choose tough plants to cope with these conditions—succulents from deserts accustomed to cold nights, or hardy plants that tolerate frost—in order to keep the warmth in your welcome.

Sparrmannia africana, **p.157**

Tolmiea menziesii 'Taff's Gold', **p.166**

Cordyline australis, **p.58**

Streptocarpus hybrids

Cape primrose

The majority of streptocarpus offered for sale are large-flowered hybrids, although you may occasionally come across species such as *S. saxorum*, whose trailing stems carry small, almost round leaves and attractive flowers, or the extraordinary *S. wenlandii*, with one huge leaf up to 28 in (70 cm) long—but be warned, this plant dies after flowering. The hybrids come in a wide range of colors including white, pink, blue, and rich ruby, and are among the prettiest and gentlest of houseplants.

HOW MUCH LIGHT
Provide good light, but not direct sunlight.

ROOM TEMPERATURE
Normal room temperature will keep the plants in flower all year. Flowering stops below 55°F (13°C).

WHEN TO WATER
Water freely during the warmer months, allowing the top of the potting mix to dry out between waterings. Water sparingly when temperatures are low.

SURVIVAL STRATEGY
Standing the plant on a tray of damp pebbles to raise humidity will help prevent the leaves from browning due to dry air (see p.178). Provide a half-strength high-potash liquid fertilizer every 3–4 weeks. Remove spent flowers to encourage more blooms.

SIZE
10 in/25 cm

SITE
Tabletop display

Stromanthe sanguinea 'Tricolor'

Stromanthe

Carrying its leaves at a jaunty, almost horizontal angle, this is a plant that exudes confidence. Its other chief attraction comes from the vibrant red leaf undersides, which contrast well with the mottled upper surfaces. Keep the foliage clean to make the most of the glossy surface. You can split the eventual thicket of shoots in spring; pot them up to provide new plants.

Leaf undersides are streaked with red.

HOW MUCH LIGHT
Keep out of direct light. Bright filtered light is ideal.

ROOM TEMPERATURE
Normal temperature is adequate. High temperatures without humidity will cause leaf browning.

WHEN TO WATER
Keep the potting mix moist in the growing season but ease off during winter, allowing the soil to dry slightly before watering.

SURVIVAL STRATEGY
During the growing season, apply a half-strength balanced liquid fertilizer every two weeks. The cool, semi-shaded conditions in which I grow this plant help it cope with low humidity. Warmer temperatures would encourage faster growth but necessitate higher humidity.

SIZE
19 in/47 cm

SITE
Hallway

Syngonium podophyllum

Goosefoot plant

The tall, gangly original plain green form of goosefoot is rarely seen, having been replaced by a range of compact plants with various variegated leaf patterns. The speckled varieties remind me of leaves affected by red spider mite—which keeps me sitting on the fence regarding this plant. The leaves of mature specimens become divided and lobed, providing much more visual interest. All syngoniums enjoy plenty of humidity.

HOW MUCH LIGHT
Bright filtered light. Keep out of direct sunlight.

ROOM TEMPERATURE
Normal room temperature, 64–75°F (18–24°C). Requires higher humidity in warmer temperatures.

WHEN TO WATER
Keep the potting mix moist year-round, but allow it to dry slightly between waterings.

SURVIVAL STRATEGY
Grow up a moss pole or let it trail from a shelf or basket. Feed regularly when in growth. If your houseplants are prone to red spider mite, check this plant carefully— the leaf patterns resemble the symptoms of mite infestation and may mask an attack (see p.187).

SIZE
13 in/33 cm

SITE
Hanging basket; bright shelf

Tillandsia cyanea
Pink quill

A curious but striking plant. The flower head is flattened into a fanlike arrangement and the flowers emerge from between the "scales" or overlapping bracts. Up to 20 flowers appear individually, and while each is short-lived, they are produced over a long period, sometimes lasting 10 weeks. Once flowering is finished, the rosette of leaves bearing the flower spike dies. It is replaced by offshoots, which may be used for propagation, or left to mature and flower on the plant.

DRIP-FEEDING Tillandsias have sparse roots, which are just enough to anchor the plant. Water and nutrients are also taken in by the leaves, which means that they will benefit from regular misting.

HOW MUCH LIGHT
Grow in good light but out of direct scorching sunshine.

ROOM TEMPERATURE
A year-round temperature of 64–77°F (18–25°C) is ideal, but it tolerates a winter minimum of 57°F (14°C).

WHEN TO WATER
Waterlogging means certain death, so a free-draining pot and potting mix are crucial. In warmer months, either mist frequently so water runs down into soil, or, when it is almost dry, dunk it in soft water at room temperature and drain thoroughly. Water sparingly in winter.

SURVIVAL STRATEGY
During the growing season it benefits from a monthly application of a quarter-strength balanced liquid fertilizer applied either via a misting spray or in the dunking water. Provide as humid an atmosphere as possible.

SIZE
10 in/26 cm

SITE
Bathroom

Tolmiea menziesii 'Taff's Gold'

Piggyback plant

This is a perfectly hardy plant that has become established as a very attractive houseplant for cool and shady conditions. It owes its common name to the young plants that form at the point where the stalk meets the leaf blade. If you detach them with the leaf, they will root and form new plants when pressed into the soil surface. The tall flower stalks bear small flowers of exquisite detail, but if flowers are produced at all indoors, they are best removed to keep the plant looking neat.

HOW MUCH LIGHT
Likes bright filtered light to semi-shade. Low light levels and warm conditions lead to straggly growth.

ROOM TEMPERATURE
Keep cool; this hardy plant is used to an outdoor life, so high indoor winter temperatures cause drawn growth.

WHEN TO WATER
Keep the potting mix moist throughout the growing season.

SURVIVAL STRATEGY
Outside, tolmieas would normally experience a cold winter period, so they benefit from a few weeks of cooler temperatures when grown indoors.

SIZE
8 in/20 cm

SITE
North- or east-facing window

Tradescantia spathacea syn. *Rhoeo discolor*

Boatlily

The robust shape of this plant is not what you might expect from a tradescantia—the name is more often associated with small-leaved trailers—but a glance at the flowers confirms the relationship. Young plants start out sitting on the soil with an erect rosette of stiff leaves, but as they mature, the lower leaves are lost and a stem begins to develop.

White flowers cradled at the center of the plant.

HOW MUCH LIGHT
Enjoys bright light, but keep out of direct sun, which may scorch the leaves.

ROOM TEMPERATURE
Normal room temperature, 64–75°F (18–24°C), is adequate, with a winter minimum of 61–63°F (16–17°C).

WHEN TO WATER
Water regularly, keeping the potting mix moist but not wet during the growing period. Keep only just moist during cooler winter months. Overwatering in winter will cause the roots and stem to rot.

SURVIVAL STRATEGY
Good humidity is important to avoid browned leaves or leaf tips. Group with other plants, or stand it on a tray of damp pebbles (see p.178). The higher the temperature, the greater the amount of humidity needed. Fertilize regularly during the spring and summer.

SIZE
21 in/52 cm

SITE
Bright living room

Tradescantia zebrina

Wandering Jew

A delightful, easy-to-grow plant that can be trained up a small frame or allowed to spill out of its pot and trail downward. The leaves are marked with two silver stripes—which catch the light with a sparkling glint— and their purple undersides create a perfect contrast. And for bonus points, it will occasionally produce small pink flowers.

Striped silvery-green leaves are purple beneath.

HOW MUCH LIGHT
Bright light will give you the best leaf coloring and encourage flowering, but avoid direct scorching sunlight.

ROOM TEMPERATURE
Normal room temperature, 64–75°F (18–24°C), is ideal with a minimum of 54°F (12°C) in winter.

WHEN TO WATER
Keep potting mix moist when actively growing. Water less in winter, but do not allow to dry out.

SURVIVAL STRATEGY
Long trailing shoots may lose their leaves and become straggly at the base. Either pinch out the growing tips to keep the plant bushy, or tuck the trailing shoots back into the pot, where they will root and form a new plant with fresh leaves. Fertilize regularly in summer.

SIZE
14 in/35 cm

SITE
Hanging basket

Vriesea splendens
Flaming sword

Surely one of the most striking plants for the home. The broad, slightly rolled leaves are banded deep purple with shiny undersides that gleam like richly polished wood. The scarlet flower spike is held atop a sturdy stem, and colorful bracts are tightly pressed together in a flattened flower head; even if small yellow flowers failed to squeeze themselves from between the bracts, the brilliant spike would still carry the day. The spike lasts for many weeks but eventually turns brown; cut it off near the base. It's much tougher than the exotic appearance suggests, being happy at room temperature, and easily maintained.

DRINKING CUP The center of the plant forms a remarkably watertight cup, which you should top off at regular intervals throughout the plant's growing season.

☀ HOW MUCH LIGHT
For good leaf color and flowers, it needs bright light with 2–3 hours of direct sun, but not scorching heat.

🌡 ROOM TEMPERATURE
When in growth, 64–82°F (18–28°C) is ideal, with a winter minimum of 59°F (15°C). Keep humidity high.

💧 WHEN TO WATER
Water regularly into the central cup formed by the leaves and keep the potting mix moist when the plant is actively growing. In cooler periods of the year, when growth is slowed, keep soil just moist. Be careful not to overwater at this time.

✋ SURVIVAL STRATEGY
During the growing season, provide half-strength balanced liquid fertilizer every month. Pot in orchid mix or other free-draining mix. Rosettes that have flowered will die back over a period of months. Offsets from the leaf axils will take the place of the withering rosette.

📏 SIZE
28 in/70 cm

🏠 SITE
East- or west-facing window

Zantedeschia hybrids
Calla lily

Zantedeschias do not flower for long periods, but the brevity of the display is well compensated for by the beauty and elegance of the flowers. There is a wide range of colors available, from rich orangey-yellow to purple, pink, and white. The flowering season runs from early summer to midsummer, after which plants die back for a dormant period. You can bring them back into growth during winter or early spring, ready to flower again. Alternatively, flowering plants can be used for a short-term display and then discarded.

Z. elliottiana

HOW MUCH LIGHT
When the plant is in leaf, provide bright light, including 1–2 hours of direct sunlight.

ROOM TEMPERATURE
Best at normal temperature 64–75°F (18–24°C); the flowers last longer in cooler conditions, around 61°F (16°C).

WHEN TO WATER
Keep moist when in active growth, but after flowering, allow to dry out. Apply a balanced liquid fertilizer every two weeks when plants are in full leaf and active growth.

SURVIVAL STRATEGY
Gradually dry off the plant after flowering, remove the collapsing leaves, and keep the dormant rhizome dry. Repot when new shoots emerge through the potting mix in winter or early spring, and gradually increase watering as leaves develop.

SIZE
20 in/50 cm

SITE
Conservatory

Plant care

Plantcare | Potting

As plants get bigger, the roots become congested and may eventually need a bigger pot with more soil to satisfy their need for water and nutrients. Equally, you may just want to move your plant into a more attractive container. "Potting up" to a larger size is a simple task if you follow a few basic rules about drainage and soil. Don't be tempted to pot into a vastly bigger container, since waterlogging may result.

Choosing soil

Most plants are happy in sterile, multipurpose potting mix (don't use garden soil). Special mixes are available for plants with particular needs: fast-draining and gritty for cacti; ericaceous for acid-lovers, like camellias; and very coarse-textured for plants that dislike wet roots at any time, like orchids.

Adding extra nutrients

Multipurpose potting mixes have a limited supply of nutrients, which are soon exhausted. Repotting provides the ideal opportunity to give the soil a boost by mixing fertilizer granules into the fresh mix. Through the effects of water and temperature, the granules release a steady supply of food to your plant over the whole growing season. Fertilizers come in several different forms but basically work the same way.

Granules should simply be mixed evenly into the potting mix.

Moisture-retentive multipurpose mix

Sticks of fertilizer (above left) and clusters of granules (above) may be pressed into the soil surface (left). They gradually release their nutrients over several months: every time you water the plant, the roots receive a boost, and old potting mix is revitalized.

Gritty, light cactus mix

Coarse, low-nutrient orchid mix

How to repot your plant

Repotting gives plants a new lease on life and encourages new, healthy shoots. Use a pot just 1 in (2–3 cm) wider than the old one. Ideally, repot your plant at the start of the growing season or when the plant is in active growth. Avoid repotting when the plant is dormant in winter, since damaged roots may rot on inactive plants.

1 A 1-in (2–3-cm) layer of styrofoam pieces or pot or crockery shards across the hole provides necessary spaces for good drainage, and helps prevent waterlogging.

1 in (2 cm) allowed for watering

Root ball sits on a layer of soil

Styrofoam

2 Put a layer of potting mix in the bottom of the pot to bring the top of the root ball 1 in (2–3 cm) below the rim. This will provide just enough space for watering.

3 Carefully feed in the potting mix around the plant. Firm it in gently, but avoid over-compacting the soil, since this hinders drainage and drives out all the air.

Layer of mulch

Compost fills sides

4 Add a layer of mulch for an attractive finish. It reduces evaporation, but makes checking for water more difficult. You'll need to scrape it away from the potting mix to check moisture levels.

Top-dressing

Plants in large pots are often too large or heavy to remove for repotting and may already be in as big a pot as you want. To keep them healthy, apply a top-dressing of fresh potting mix each year in spring.

1 Remove the top 1 in (2–3 cm) of soil. Do not worry unduly about damaging fine roots.

2 Spread a 1-in (2–3-cm) layer of moist soil mixed with fertilizer over the surface.

Plantcare | Where to put your plant

The best way to make sure your plant stays healthy and performs well is to match its needs to a suitable position in your home. A plant may be aesthetically pleasing in a certain spot, but if the light and temperature conditions are inappropriate, and if you fail to meet other specific needs, such as humidity, it will soon lose its appeal as it becomes more and more sickly-looking.

Effect of temperature

You are very unlikely to maintain a constant temperature in every part of your house. Cold drafts may blast through windows or doors that are regularly opened; a basement may provide relative winter cool; and an unventilated conservatory may experience blistering summer heat. In every case, an awareness of the conditions will help you choose suitable plants.

Cacti are very robust. A resistance to hot days and cold nights means they are able to take fluctuating conservatory conditions.

Plants behind drawn curtains in winter can get caught in a trap of cold air. Avoid excluding them from a heated room.

Ways to increase humidity

Humidity refers to the amount of water in the air. The levels experienced by plants in their habitats often govern their needs: keep a plant from the tropical forest in dry air and its leaves will shrivel. Given too much humidity, plants from dry climates are likely to rot. Most houseplants are pretty tolerant, and you'll only need to raise humidity levels when it's hot to prevent plant stress.

The bathroom is often the most humid room in the house, due to hot baths or steamy showers. It's the ideal place for plants that demand higher humidity.

Plants give off moisture as part of their natural processes, so a group of plants creates a small area of higher humidity.

Mist leaves with water

Pebble layer is ideally as wide as the plant's spread

Keep water level just below the top of the pebbles

Stand a plant on a tray of moist pebbles to raise humidity through evaporation. Misting increases humidity, but you'll have to do it several times a day for it to be effective.

How much light?

Plant labels usually indicate the need for "direct," "bright filtered," or "medium" light, but what exactly does this mean? Light varies within the room, and at different times of year: plants unable to cope with hot direct summer sun may benefit from a site near the window in winter to better absorb weaker light. Plants need light to survive and naturally turn toward it; although twisting plants around every few days prevents lopsided growth, it is not ideal, and some may suffer bud drop if the angle changes. It's best to make sure plants are correctly lit.

Plants in poor light may lean disfiguringly toward it; turn them to ensure even growth.

Direct light: the plant receives full sun for much of the day. Strong summer sun, especially at midday, is too much for most plants.

Bright, filtered light: sunlight through a mesh curtain or gauze blind remains bright but is far less likely to scorch the leaves of your plant.

Medium light: a position farther into the room, away from the glare of a window, suits many foliage plants that enjoy good light.

Low light: few plants enjoy shady conditions where there is no direct source of light; those with large, dark green leaves are most likely to cope.

Boosting light levels

You can increase the amount of light available in rooms with little or no direct sun. Light, reflective walls and surfaces as well as paler-colored furnishings will help to brighten a room. Keep the curtains drawn well back to allow as much light in as possible, and make sure your windows are clean. Consider whitewashing exterior walls or fences close to the house to bounce light into the room.

Keep leaves clean to allow maximum light penetration. Use a soft, damp cloth to remove grime, or wash dirt away in a tepid shower.

Cacti look scruffy when covered in dust, which also blocks out much-needed light. Clean between the spines with a paintbrush or cotton swab.

Plantcare | Support

Properly cared for, plants are going to grow—some very vigorously—and sooner or later they will need your help to keep them looking good or within bounds. Time spent trimming or training is rewarded with shapely plants, and a greater understanding of how they grow.

How to train up a moss pole

Moss poles are ideal for climbers like cheese plants (*Monstera*). You can either buy them, or make your own by wrapping moss around a plastic tube and binding it with fishing line. Keep moist to encourage aerial roots to penetrate the moss.

1 It's easy to tame a wayward monstera upward. Using a spoon handle, make a small hole in the soil, avoiding major roots, and push pole firmly into the pot.

2 Although it seems like a tangled mess, this plant has two main stems. Gently twist each stem around the pole in turn, taking care not to break them.

3 Keep stems in contact with the pole as much as possible and tie them in with soft garden twine. Use a shoelace knot that is easy to adjust as you maneuver stems.

4 Step back regularly to check your work as you tie in the stems, to be sure the plant is well balanced—it not only looks good but makes the finished plant stable.

Making loops

Most trailing or climbing plants can be "formalized" on a frame to give them an entirely new look. Here, I have used a bushy trailing ivy, but plants like jasmine, passion flower, cissus, or even *Tradescantia zebrina* can be treated this way.

1 Provide a suitably-sized circle of sturdy wire, ideally galvanized or coated, leaving two long straight "legs" on the end, and push them down into the soil just inside the rim of the pot.

2 Taking the longest stems first, wind them around the wire from both ends of the loop. Gradually weave other stems into the loop to create a robust-looking circle of greenery.

3 Once you are happy with the overall effect, trim off all the other trailing shoots. Keep it neat and tidy by clipping over with scissors or pruners and bending new shoots into the loop.

Keeping plants in shape

As plants develop, they may lose their shape, and in the case of climbers, they can start to grow away from their supports. Keep on top of tweaking, trimming, and tying in shoots to ensure that your plants continue looking their best.

Many climbers, like this passion flower, grow vigorously, but you can contain them by training new shoots back on themselves along the framework. It's best to do this while the shoots are still young and pliable. Occasionally cutting out old shoots is a job that will test your patience, but it helps to maintain your plant's youth and vigor.

Formal shapes need regular clipping. On foliage plants, this is straightforward—most can be cut back at any time during their growing period. With flowering plants, if you are unsure, it's best to wait until flowering is over before cutting back. This olive is being pruned when it is easy to see where the flowers are.

Deadheading

Many plants stop flowering once they have set seed, which means removing spent blooms encourages new buds to form. Plants with large flowers like this hibiscus look neater with old flowers removed, and this also keeps fallen petals from resting on and rotting the foliage. Cut off as much of the flower stalk as possible to prevent rotting.

Creating a standard

Growing a plant on a single stem can give it a completely new character and adds another dimension to plant groupings.

Here I have used an abutilon, but you can achieve the same effect with lantana, pachira, citrus or, with extra support, ivy.

1 Choose a plant with a strong, centrally placed and unbranching stem that runs right to the top of the plant to train as a standard.

2 Cut out any competing upright shoots, then remove the leaves and any sideshoots from the lower half of the plant.

3 Thin stems need support. Avoid "throttling" the stem by tying string around the cane first and then loosely around the stem.

4 When plant reaches the desired height, pinch out the leading tip for a bushy head. Rub off any young shoots that sprout on the bare stem.

Plantcare | What's wrong?

There are three main causes of ill-health in plants: pests and diseases, incorrect watering, and poor siting. The problem is that plants often react in similar ways to all these events with yellowing or browning leaves, wilting stems, or falling flowers and foliage. So how do you know what's wrong? The first thing to remember is: Don't Panic. Avoid jumping to conclusions, learn to read your plants, and try to work out what's really bothering them. In the case of pests and diseases, your best defense is to exercise vigilance, and deal with trouble before it gets out of hand.

Poor begonia! Lack of fertilizer has turned foliage yellow. Debris and old leaves have been left to rot on the soil. Rot has spread to the stems, causing more dieback. Underwatering has made it wilt.

Yellowing leaves

• **A sign of age**
Low leaves often turn yellow and drop off as plants grow: they are shed as they are inefficient.
DON'T WORRY, this is natural. Remove old leaves as they fade to keep the plant looking neat.

• **Low temperatures**
Plants accustomed to warmth may become stressed if temperatures fall. This causes leaves to yellow, and may be accompanied by brown spots.
MOVE PLANTS to a warmer environment to recover.

• **Undernourishment**
Nitrogen is essential to produce chlorophyll. If soil fails to provide enough nitrogen, plants are unable to make chlorophyll or collect light energy. Plants short of nitrogen move it to where it is needed most, often the top of the plant, causing lower leaves to fade.
REGULAR FERTILIZING with balanced fertilizer prevents poor nutrition.

• **Hard water**
Some plants need nonalkaline conditions. Hard water raises the soil's alkalinity, making iron and nitrogen unavailable.
USE SOFT WATER and a fertilizer formulated for acid-loving plants.

• **Underwatering**
Plants kept dry cannot take up water and fail to get the nutrients water brings, leading to undernourishment and yellow lower leaves.
CHECK REGULARLY for dry soil and water accordingly.

• **Overwatering**
Waterlogged roots cannot function properly and do not provide plants with essential water or nutrients, so the leaves yellow and stems wilt despite the potting mix being moist.
DO NOT LEAVE plants standing in water-filled saucers. See p.182.

Leaf, flower, or bud drop

• **Sudden temperature changes**
These can shock plants into shedding buds and leaves to conserve energy.
PROVIDE more stable conditions

• **The angle of light has changed**
As plants adjust to the new light source buds become detached.
AVOID turning these plants and make sure they are correctly lit.

• **Underwatering**
The plant sheds leaves and buds to conserve moisture.
CHECK soil and water plant.

Scorched leaves

• **Too much heat**
Hot conditions especially when combined with inadequate water cause scorched leaves.
REDUCE temperature, increase watering, and raise humidity.

• **Not enough humidity**
Leaves lose water faster than it travels into the leaf, causing their tips and edges to dry out and turn brown.
MOVE PLANTS to a more humid area or mist to raise humidity.

Pests and diseases

Adult vine weevils are slow, flightless creatures that come out at night and chew notches in leaf margins. They are easily caught and picked off.

Vine weevil grubs eat away at plant roots, unnoticed until the plant wilts. Chemical or biological nematode controls are available.

Soft, crowded, damaged, or wet plant tissue is at risk from attacks of gray mold. Prevent it by removing fallen leaves and practice good hygiene.

Red spider mites are tiny, but speckling and webbing on leaves indicate their presence. Use biological and chemical controls.

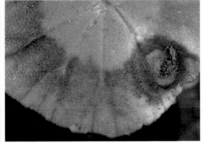

Fallen petals left lying on foliage cause molds to develop. Pelargoniums are particularly prone to this problem. Deadhead regularly.

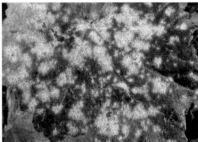

Powdery mildew is generally a begonia problem, and only on plants stressed by drought or heat. Improve conditions and spray with fungicide.

Aphids increase rapidly in warm conditions. Rub them off or use chemical and biological controls.

Mealy bugs hide in leaves and stems. Rub them off, dig them out, or use biological controls.

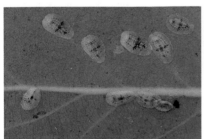

Soft scale insects are easily spotted on stems and leaves. Rub off or use biological controls.

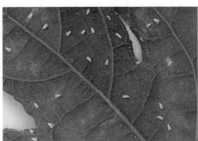

Whitefly. Best controlled with biological controls or chemicals to kill all stages of their life cycle.

Sooty mold is nature's way of telling you have a problem with aphids, scale insects, whitefly or mealy bugs, all of which exude a sticky waste on which the mold grows. Cure your insect problem and you cure your sooty mold problem.

Index | Plant categories

This list is intended as a guide to help you find an appropriate plant for your site, or one with particular characteristics.

AIR FRESHENERS

Aglaonema	24
Chlorophytum	52
Dieffenbachia	72
Dracaena	76
Dypsis	78
Epipremnum	80
Ficus	86
Hedera	95
Musa	118
Nephrolepis	120
Rhapis	142
Schlumbergera	149
Spathiphyllum	160
Syngonium	164

BATHROOM

Adiantum	20
Aglaonema	24
Alocasia	25
Aspidistra	30
Asplenium	31
Begonia	34
Caladium	39
Calathea	40
Caryota	48
Chamaedorea	50
Chlorophytum	52
Ctenanthe	62
Cymbidium	67
Cyperus	68
Cyrtomium	69
Davallia	70
Dendrobium	71
Dieffenbachia	72
Epipremnum	80
Fittonia	90
Howea	99
Impatiens	104
Isolepis	105
Monstera	115
Nematanthus	119
Nephrolepis	120
Pachira	124
Paphiopedilum	125

Phalaenopsis	133
Philodendron	134
Phoenix	136
Platycerium	138
Pteris	140
Rhapis	142
Saintpaulia	146
Sansevieria	147
Schefflera	148
Selaginella	151
Soleirolia	154
Spathiphyllum	160
Stromanthe	163
Syngonium	164
Tillandsia	165
Tolmiea	166
Tradescantia zebrina	168

CLIMBING & TRAILING

Bougainvillea	37
Ceropegia	49
Chlorophytum	52
Cissus	54
Epipremnum	80
Gynura	94
Hedera	95
Hoya	100
Jasminum	106
Lotus	112
Mandevilla	113
Monstera	115
Nematanthus	119
Passiflora	126
Philodendron	134
Plumbago	139
Senecio	152
Sollya	156
Stephanotis	161
Syngonium	164
Tradescantia zebrina	168

COLD-TOLERANT

Adiantum	20
Agave	23
Aloe	26
Aspidistra	30
Campanula	44
Ceropegia	49
Chamaerops	51

Chrysanthemum	53
Cordyline	58
Crassula	59
Cycas	65
Cyclamen	66
Cyrtomium	69
Fatsia	84
Graptopetalum	92
Grevillea	93
Hedera	95
Isolepis	105
Jasminum	106
Lavandula	111
Olea	123
Pachira	124
Passiflora	126
Pericallis	132
Phoenix	136
Punica	141
Rhododendron	143
Schefflera	148
Soleirolia	154
Sollya	156
Sparrmannia	157
Tolmiea	166
Yucca	170
Zantedeschia	172

COLORED FOLIAGE

Acalypha	19
Aeonium	22
Begonia	34
Codiaeum	57
Fittonia	90
Gynura	94
Hemigraphis	96
Hypoestes	101
Peperomia	128
Philodendron	134
Pilea	137
Soleirolia	154
Solenostemon	155
Tolmiea	166
Tradescantia spathacea	167

CONSERVATORY

Abutilon	18
Aeonium	22
Agave	23

Aloe   26
Ananas   27
Billbergia   36
Bougainvillea   37
Brugmansia   38
Callisia   42
Camellia   43
Capsicum   45
Ceropegia   49
Chamaerops   51
Citrus   55
Curcuma   64
Cycas   65
Cordyline   58
Crassula   59
Echeveria   79
Euphorbia tirucalli   82
Ferocactus   85
Graptopetalum   92
Hibiscus   97
Hoya   100
Kalanchoe   108
Lantana   110
Lavandula   111
Lotus   112
Mandevilla   113
Musa   118
Nolina   122
Olea   123
Passiflora   126
Pelargonium   127
Phoenix   136
Plumbago   139
Punica   141
Rhododendron   143
Schlumbergera   149
Sedum   150
Solanum   153
Sollya   156
Stephanotis   161
Yucca   170

DRAMATIC SHAPE

Aechmea   21
Aeonium   22
Agave   23
Alocasia   25
Aspidistra   30
Caladium   39
Caryota   48

Chamaedorea   50
Chamaerops   51
Codiaeum   57
Cordyline   58
Ctenanthe   62
Cycas   65
Cyperus   68
Dizygotheca   73
Dracaena   76
Euphorbia tirucalli   82
Ficus   86
Monstera   115
Musa   118
Nephrolepis   120
Nolina   122
Philodendron   134
Phoenix   136
Platycerium   138
Rhapis   142
Sansevieria   147
Schefflera   148
Sparrmannia   157
Stromanthe   163
Tillandsia   165
Vriesea   169
Yucca   170
Zamioculcas   171

FLOWERS

Abutilon   18
Acalypha   19
Begonia   34
Billbergia   36
Bougainvillea   37
Brugmansia   38
Camellia   43
Campanula   44
Chrysanthemum   53
Clivia   56
Cuphea   63
Curcuma   64
Cyclamen   66
Cymbidium   67
Dendrobium   71
Echeveria   79
Euphorbia pulcherrima   81
Exacum   83
Gardenia   91
Graptopetalum   92
Hibiscus   97

Hippeastrum   98
Hoya   100
Impatiens   104
Jasminum   106
Justicia   107
Kalanchoe   108
Lantana   110
Lavandula   111
Lotus   112
Mandevilla   113
Nematanthus   119
Nertera   121
Paphiopedilum   125
Passiflora   126
Pelargonium   127
Pericallis   132
Phalaenopsis   133
Plumbago   139
Punica   141
Rhododendron   143
Saintpaulia   146
Schlumbergera   149
Solanum   153
Sollya   156
Spathiphyllum   160
Stephanotis   161
Streptocarpus   162
Tillandsia   165
Vriesea   169
Zantedeschia   172

LARGE PLANTS

Abutilon   18
Bougainvillea   37
Brugmansia   38
Caryota   48
Chamaedorea   50
Chamaerops   51
Curcuma   64
Cyperus   68
Dieffenbachia   72
Dizygotheca   73
Dracaena   76
Epipremnum   80
Euphorbia tirucalli   82
Fatsia   84
Ficus   86
Howea   99
Hibiscus   97
Jasminum   106

Index | Plant categories

Mandevilla 113
Monstera 115
Musa 118
Olea 123
Pachira 124
Passiflora 126
Philodendron 134
Phoenix 136
Plumbago 139
Schefflera 148
Sollya 156
Sparrmannia 157
Stephanotis 161
Stromanthe 163
Syngonium 164
Yucca 170
Zamioculcas 171

LOW LIGHT
Aspidistra 30
Adiantum 20
Cyrtomium 69
Fatsia 84
Hedera 95
Maranta 114
Rhododendron 143
Sansevieria 147

ORCHIDS
Cymbidium 67
Dendrobium 71
Paphiopedilum 125
Phalaenopsis 133

PALMS
Caryota 48
Chamaedorea 50
Chamaerops 51
Dypsis 78
Howea 99
Phoenix 136
Rhapis 142

PATTERNED FOLIAGE
Aglaonema 24
Alocasia 25
Ananas 27
Begonia 34

Billbergia 36
Caladium 39
Calathea 40
Ceropegia 49
Chlorophytum 52
Codiaeum 57
Cordyline 58
Ctenanthe 62
Cuphea 63
Cyclamen 66
Dieffenbachia 72
Dracaena 76
Ficus 86
Hedera 95
Hibiscus 97
Hypoestes 101
Maranta 114
Peperomia 128
Philodendron 134
Pilea 137
Sansevieria 147
Schefflera 148
Senecio 152
Solenostemon 155
Stromanthe 163
Syngonium 164
Tolmiea 166
Tradescantia zebrina 168
Vriesea 169

SCENTED FLOWERS
Brugmansia 38
Citrus 55
Gardenia 91
Jasminum 106
Lavandula 111
Stephanotis 161

SUCCULENTS
Aeonium 22
Agave 23
Aloe 26
Crassula 59
Echeveria 79
Euphorbia tirucalli 82
Ferocactus 85
Graptopetalum 92
Kalanchoe 108
Sansevieria 147

Sedum 150
Zamioculcas 171

TEXTURE
Aeonium 22
Agave 23
Cycas 65
Crassula 59
Davallia 70
Dypsis 78
Ferocactus 85
Ficus 86
Gynura 94
Kalanchoe 108
Lavandula 111
Lotus 112
Nephrolepis 120
Nertera 121
Peperomia 128
Philodendron 134

Index │ Common names

A B

Aeonium	22
African hemp	157
African violet	146
Agave	23
Aglaonema	24
Aluminum plant	137
Amaryllis	98
Angel wings	39
Angels' trumpets	38
Azalea	143
Baby's tears	154
Banana	118
Bead plant	121
Begonia	34
Bird's-nest fern	31
Bluebell creeper	156
Boatlily	167
Boston fern	120
Bougainvillea	37
Busy Lizzie	104
Butterfly palm	78

C

Cabbage palm	58
Calamondin orange	55
Calla lily	172
Camellia	43
Canary Island date palm	136
Cape ivy	152
Cape leadwort	139
Cape primrose	162
Cast-iron plant	30
Chenille plant	19
Chili pepper	45
Christmas cactus	149
Christmas cherry	153
Chrysanthemum	53
Cigar flower	63
Coleus	155
Common staghorn fern	138
Cretan brake	140
Croton	57
Cyclamen	66
Cymbidium	67

D E F

Dendrobium	71
Devil's ivy	80
Devil's tongue	85
Donkey's tail	150
Dumb cane	72
Dwarf fan palm	51
Echeveria	79
Elephant ear	25
English ivy	95
False aralia	73
Fishtail palm	48
Flaming sword	169
Flamingo flower	28
Florists' cineraria	132
Flowering maple	18
Foxtail fern	29

G H

Gardenia	91
Geranium	127
Goosefoot plant	164
Grape ivy	54
Graptopetalum	92
Hare's-foot fern	70
Hearts on a string	49
Hemigraphis	96

I J K L

Jade plant	59
Japanese aralia	84
Japanese holly fern	69
Japanese sago palm	65
Jasmine	106
Kaffir lily	56
Kalanchoe	108
Lantana	110
Lavender	111

M

Madagascar dragon tree	76
Madagascar jasmine	161
Maidenhair fern	20
Malabar chestnut	124
Mandevilla	113
Miniature fan palm	142
Moth orchid	133
Mother-in-law's tongue	147

N O P Q

Nemanthus	119
Nerve plant	90
Never-never plant	62
Olive	123
Parlor palm	50
Parrot's beak	112
Partridge-breast aloe	26
Passion flower	126
Peace lily	160
Peacock plant	40
Pencil cactus	82
Peperomia	128
Persian violet	83
Philodendron	134
Piggyback plant	166
Pineapple	27
Pink quill	165
Poinsettia	91
Polka-dot plant	101
Pomegranate	141
Ponytail palm	122
Prayer plant	114
Purple velvet plant	94
Purple waffle plant	96
Queen's tears	36

R S

Rose of China	97
Rubber plant	86
Selaginella	151
Sentry palm	99
Shrimp plant	107
Siam tulip	64
Silk oak	93
Slender club-rush	105
Slipper orchid	125
Spider plant	52
Star-of-Bethlehem	44
Swiss cheese plant	115

U V W Y Z

Umbrella plant	68
Umbrella tree	148
Vase plant	21
Wandering Jew	168
Wax flower	100
Yucca	170
Zamioculcas	171

Acknowledgments

AUTHOR'S ACKNOWLEDGMENTS
A very big thank you to Kate Kenyan at the Flowers and Plants Association, whose help and cooperation in locating, collecting, and delivering plants was massive and made life so much easier.

An extremely big and special thanks to the DK team of Helen Fewster and Rachael Smith, whose professionalism has made the whole project run smoothly and efficiently and, best of all, it has always been done with a smile.

Big thanks also to Sian Irvine for her hospitality and chocolate cookies.

Many thanks to Fibrex Nursery, Pebworth, Warwickshire for help identifying Pelargonium cultivars. Thank you also to Gwen Dixon for the loan of plant material.

The publishers also wish to thank Ali Edney and Juliette Hopkins.

Thanks also to: Crocus.co.uk; Chelsea Gardener; R.K. Alliston; and Marston & Langinger, 192 Ebury Street, London, SW1W 8UP (+44 020 7881 5717) for the loan of their pots.

PHOTOGRAPHY CREDITS
The publisher would like to thank the following for their kind permission to reproduce their photographs:

Abbreviations key: a=above, b=below, c=center, l=left; r=right, t=top
Alamy Images: Holt Studios International Ltd 187tr, 187ca, 187cra.
Ardea.com: Steve Hopkin 187tl.
Photos Horticultural: 187cla, 187br; B.T. 187clb.

COMMISSIONED PHOTOGRAPHS
Craig Knowles: 165 inset, 167 inset, 181 bl, 181 bc.
Verity Welstead: 15, 60, 61l, 61tr, 89bl, 103t, 116, 117tr, 131tl, 145tr, 176tc, 179c, 179cr.
All other images © Dorling Kindersley. For further information see: www.dkimages.com